First page and dedication

I would like to dedicate this book to my family; you have given me everything.

"All the happiness in this world is as a result of wanting other people to be happy, all the unhappiness in this world is as a result of wanting yourself to be solely happy".

Bodhisattva Shantideva

Acknowledgements

I would like to thank many people for their time, effort and dedication. Your contribution and advice has helped me put this entire project together.

Jason Mcgill, Gerry Mckay, James Rees, Lisa Jones, Peter Britton, Owain Morgan, Becky Li, Andrew Cockel, Deborah Smith, Matthew Hapgood, Robert Bambridge, Ceri Davies, Lucy Evans, Jane Down, Leo Velensek, Pat Craven, James Harper, Richard Blackwell, Jeff Tildesley, Georgina Runnalls, Karen Powell, Tom Davies, Laura Richards, Maxim Collins, William Deacon, Liz Thomas, Sarah Morgan, Rev Mark Thomas, Katie Oram, Lezley Evans, Geshe Kelsang Gyatso, Julie Gatters and Dave Gatters, Tom Anderson, Neil Evans, Phil Cooper, Adam Richards, Gabrielle Harvey, Paul Harvey, Jan Battrick, Phillip Thomas, Peter Britton and Lorraine Aston.

INTRODUCTION

In 2001 I became a police officer with the South Wales Police and since that time I have been fortunate enough to be involved in many people's lives. Police work opened up my limited life experience and I became an authority figure overnight. That's what some people choose to see when they see a police officer. My experience is different; forget the uniform, fast cars and flashing blue lights. I have had many insights into the nature of human behaviour. The people I have met have told their story and I have listened.

One day I was trying to make sense of all the experiences that I have had. I considered the larger picture and came to realise that bullying was one of the main causes of many people's personal problems. I was fortunate to discover those causes when exposed to a variety of bullying. Bullying is all around us and affects us all; it's just called different things in different circumstances. Society dilutes bullying by calling it a different name.

Domestic violence: a man who thinks nothing of hitting his partner in front of the children, a man who belittles her at every opportunity, who controls her and ruins her confidence. Isn't this bullying? In the UK, the police get called to 1,300 incidents per day. In fact domestic violence accounts to 16% of total crime (British Crime Survey 2000), and most of it goes unreported. This is just the tip of the iceberg. A woman might suffer 35 separate incidents of abuse before she contacts the police.

The overzealous boss who criticises you for thinking out of the box, talks about you behind your back, spreads rumours about you, changes your shifts, makes you feel alone, and never asks your opinion. Workplace bullying is on the increase and it is estimated to affect one in four employees. It breaks down the team ethos at work; employers lose days due to stress and sickness.

The student who suddenly doesn't want to go to school or college, threatens suicide, self harms and uses drugs and alcohol to get away from it all. It is estimated that one million school children are bullied each week. There were 24 knife related murders in the UK until August 2008. More often than not the parents of the children bullied have experienced the same. People even commit suicide as a result of bullying.

The purpose of this book is to create an understanding of bullying and give you safe advice that will allow you to plan for, manage and avoid bullying. I have to be completely honest with you; bullying is not something that we can stop entirely, however, it is something that we can reduce. This book will help you identify situations whereby your actions can make bullying actually worse and analyses ways in which you can solve confrontational situations.

The writing of this book has come from direct experience. In the eight years of policing the streets of South Wales I have interviewed hundreds of survivors; survivors who have been battered, bruised, stalked, hounded, degraded and some have had their lives shattered. This book is a survival guide for you the victim; you are the most important part of this process.

Bullying is an absolutely horrible experience and one that can stay with you for the rest of your life. It disrupts the life force of our communities, and it is something that we need to understand and plan for. In writing this book, I cannot imagine what some of you have gone through, but it is my intention to help you minimise violent behaviour, maintaining your peace and security at all times. After all what is life without peace and happiness?

The chapters of this book are designed to be used with one another. Don't just rely on one aspect of this book. The book has sections and exercises that are aimed at improving your understanding. There is hope. With the right support and a holistic approach to bullying you can change from a victim to a survivor.

CHAPTER 1

WHAT IS A BULLY?

A bully is a person who holds the belief that they are more important than you are. They hold the opinion that they have the right to manipulate and control your thoughts, appearance and lifestyle.

A bully uses an abuse of power. The bully can use many different tactics and will insult you, mistreat you and undermine you. They will repeat their actions.

Who Is A Bully?

Anybody can be a bully. A bully isn't of a certain age, class, sex or ethnicity. A bully could be a group of people, an organisation, a community and even a country. If you hold the belief that your needs are more important than those of others and only you matter then you may develop a tendency to try to control other people. In the appropriate situation control isn't such a bad thing. Sometimes it is needed when people are at risk or the leader of a group is considering the needs of the whole group. For example a football captain sometimes needs to channel his players so that everyone benefits. The team wins and everybody can share that success. The bully becomes obvious when he stops thinking about other people. He will target his control and will continually harass you. Throughout history we have witnessed many dangerous dictators who have reigned with terror and fear. These tyrants have killed and caused misery to thousands of people. The dictator disregards the needs of the people and imposes control. He is a political bully.

Bullies come in many different guises and are not to be confused with a certain habit or trait. You have to ask your self, "What is this person's motivation?"; "What is his state of mind?" We commit bad actions when our mind is angry, tense, agitated, jealous and wicked. We act with kindness when our mind is caring and compassionate. Bullying is a state of mind and a learnt behaviour. This is a very important concept. People do have the ability to change and bullies can change if they want to. I remember avoiding a certain person at school. I saw them years later and still avoided them in the street. I questioned myself sometime later. "Can I assume she is still the same person?" I realised that my own unbalanced attitude had swayed my decision. If bullying is a state of mind, and if her mind had changed then it is logical to conclude that she is no longer a bully.

I was walking along the street one day with a student police officer. She was enjoying the thrills and spills of police life but was secretly struggling to come to terms with the reality of police work. The officer said to me, "Why are you nice to even the criminals? I can't understand. They listen to you and even admit crimes to you. I can't even get them to talk to me". I explained that "crime is a state of mind". I view the criminal as a person who suffers from an unbalanced mind. They are still human beings. They see that I genuinely care and that I am not judging them. No one likes to be judged. Not even you.

Why Do They Do It?

It's not about you. It's always about the bully. The bully's world is a reflection of his inner thoughts and feelings and how he communicates with the outside world. There are many reasons why somebody is a bully. You may hear people making many excuses for someone's behaviour. For example: his father is an alcoholic, she has had a bad upbringing, they are poor, he has been abused, his family are rich and he has been spoilt, etc. These are not really excuses but an attempt to understand why someone is doing something wrong. When we understand why somebody is behaving in a particular way we can sometimes help them. Once we understand their behaviour we can limit the damage they inflict.

Within human relationships we have to be sensitive to the idea of cause and effect. This idea can be confusing. If a bully is targeting people then there is a reason why he is doing it. Many causes added together can illicit an effect. For example: the bully woke up on the wrong side of bed, had four hours sleep, didn't eat breakfast, nearly had an accident driving to work, had a heavy workload, missed his lunch break, became moody, lost daily business, forgot to pick up the children, drank alcohol, argued with his family and upset everyone. This cycle of personal problems gains momentum and turns into bullying behaviour.

Where people get confused is that they believe that excuses are being found for the bully's behaviour. This is a misunderstanding. By learning about causes and conditions it allows us to plan for and reduce the effect. When we understand someone we are in a stronger position to act and get a positive solution to a particular problem.

Paul faces up to his bullying problem

I remember being on the school grounds of my local comprehensive school and it was break time. I was always involved in sport and would try and win at everything. I would look around the playground and think to myself, "How can I show off?". I always had a mass of energy and thinking back I was really angry. At the time I didn't know it was anger. I didn't understand it. I was bursting to get at people and wanted them to know I was in town. I would look around the school fields; everyone being happy, talking, laughing and enjoying themselves. Why wasn't I happy? Why didn't I have any friends? I felt alone and that made me mad, really mad.

I approached Matt and David. They were kicking a football and having a laugh. I could see their faces. They were frightened. I could hear myself saying, "Look at them. What a pair of wimps. Laughing and joking. I am going to make them feel just like me". I walked over to Matt and I slapped him with my right hand. I said, "I saw you looking at me. Have you got a problem?" Bang! I hit him again and again. He was cowering and covering his face. I felt really angry and full of hate. I hated the sight of him. He started to run and I just laughed. For a moment I felt powerful and victorious. I was the toughest in the yard.

A bully is an insecure person who doesn't understand his inner feelings. The bully's world view is a reflection of those feelings. In Paul's case he has a problem with his anger and cannot express himself clearly. When Paul felt angry he wasn't in control. When he saw Matt and David laughing together he immediately compared himself with Matt and David. When Paul saw the opposite of his world view he couldn't cope with the situation. The bully always wants to control the situation because he wants you to see the world from his view. The opposite of anger is peace. Laughter and happiness are part of being peaceful. Paul deliberately attacked Matt because he wanted Matt to experience what he was feeling.

After interviewing Paul about this attack he admitted to himself that he felt alone and worthless. Paul said, "When I see people happy I feel even more alone. When I bully them I feel more powerful and normal." Paul always believed that it was the other person's fault and that they were the reason for his unhappiness. The bully has a fixed way of thinking and cannot accept people's differences in opinion, culture, religion, and ideas etc. Paul is so rigid in his approach. His mind is fixed on a set of values and ideas that he believes are real and never change. He believes that these are rules, and rules can never be broken.

Our beliefs are the ideas that we have about the world. A belief is something we hold true to ourselves. Beliefs come from all around us; our parents, friends and experiences. We are moulded by the beliefs that we hold. How our beliefs are formed can be very subtle.

The bully has a very mixed up belief system and tries to apply his rational beliefs to different circumstances. Inside his mind this conflict and confusion leads to frustration.

For instance the bully may believe that:

A dog should obey its master and do what it is told

I don't believe in violence

In the right circumstances it is OK to hit a dog

A real man doesn't hit his wife

The bully's dog doesn't behave and the bully hits the dog in front of his children. What is this saying? It's saying; "If you can't get the dog under control, hit it and you will get discipline out of it, and by using violence you will achieve your aim." The bully's child has learnt that violence is OK. It gets animals to obey and it works.

Society, the media, institutions, sport and governments can reinforce the message that violence and abuse are OK. This is also called perception. Perception is a mix of beliefs, values and how we see the world from our point of view. Where we sometimes go wrong with our understanding of perception is that we are told that it is as a result of what is happening around us. This is a completely mistaken view.

Even though outside influences shape our belief system it still remains our own responsibility to make choices about what we believe. The problem the bully has is that he hasn't reflected about this fact and continues to act and behave with no consideration to his fellow human beings.

If we adopt a happy flexible belief system then the world outside also appears happy. Christmas day is a happy day; everyone we meet is happy and joyful. Except the bully as he didn't get what he wanted. It doesn't matter that his whole village is happy. If the bully does not feel happy inside then nothing else can change that. A consistent belief system is one that is based on good human qualities: patience, tolerance, kindness, trust, friendship, co-operation, respect and love. Above all it is a belief system that puts other people first and builds a sense of community.

When we are happy inside then the world also appears happy. A bully's belief of self importance comes from deep within him. Self importance can seem real and fixed. When we feel threatened we experience solid resistance in our bodies. Close your eyes and imagine that someone has upset you. If you really think about how you feel you may identify with your inner resistance. If we are deeply upset by someone or something we may feel more resistance. Human beings all feel this inner resistance. Human beings do not want to harbour these inner feelings as we all know that they are no good for us. However, the bully will choose the quickest and simplest way to get rid of these feelings. The bully will become angry. When Paul is confronted with a difference to his own values and beliefs he has to dominate and control. His inner resistance becomes real and changes into anger. Paul at this stage doesn't realise he is angry. His anger translates into abuse and eventually violence. He loses control because he needs to get rid of his pent up emotions. When he finally unleashes his frustrations he feels normal again because now he has control. The bully, however, has left a trail of destruction in his wake and has upset many people.

Have you noticed that some people argue less, are fun to be around, and seem happier? If you spend more time with these happy people you will come to realise that their outlook is flexible, and they don't consider themselves too important. The greater amount of self importance you hold about yourself will always translate into greater problems. The bully has an exaggerated sense of self importance and does not realise that his perception could be wrong.

The bully may use any excuse to punish you, very often you may hear people say, "It's because of your differences". You may be the victim of bullying for lots of reasons. Here are some excuses: you are gay, disabled, clever, ambitious, heterosexual, black, white, English, Scottish, stupid, moody, sexy, or talkative, etc. The list goes on and on and it always will go on. Never get sucked in to believing that you are a victim. You are just a normal human being doing your bit in this massively diverse world. It is always the bully's problem. The bully wants you to believe that you are useless and rubbish. If you start to believe such negative thoughts you become easier to control.

TRY THIS ONE

Go to your local paper shop and pick up a newspaper. Read the newspaper from cover to cover. Now circle with a red pen every incident involving conflict, bloodshed, etc. Cut each story out and place it on a table. Place the word "control" into the centre of the table. Now read each article again. Underline each statement that indicates some for of control. Have you realised; "bullying is a world problem"?

Can You Identify With The Following Bullies?

The husband who swears at you just because you said "hello" to another man? He is jealous and controlling. Your boss at work criticises you for being one minute late, picks holes in your work and makes jokes at your clothes. He is feeling threatened because you have fresh ideas. The class bully who singles you out because you came top of the class in your recent exam, he feels inferior because he is failing at everything and secretly lacks confidence.

TRY THIS ONE

Write down on a piece of paper what your bully is saying about you. Write down what they have done to you. Now on another piece of paper write down the insecurities that your bully has. Write about his/her feelings. Do you notice something? Read out the descriptions of your bully. Do they sound like a strong, confident person?

How Do They Do It?

The bully wants to dominate you and make you see the world as he does. He can use many ways to do this. The following characters describe abusive behaviour. Many bullies may use a variety of characters.

Mr Competitive

This type of bully uses his physical strength to dominate others. He likes competitive sports and loves to win. He will cheat to get his own way. Everything about him is aggressive. When he meets you he clasps your hand with an iron grip and stares you in the eyes and holds his stare. He walks around town like a bulldog with arms pushed out and chest ballooned. He talks with short abrupt words. When people are around him he likes to show off, and show everybody how funny he is. Everybody laughs at his jokes because they are frightened of him. He is vain and constantly looks in the mirror. Dare to challenge him and you will end up with a fist full of knuckles. He likes to bark orders at you and pretend that he is the sergeant major. He avoids conversations that have any substance and will turn around a conversation to how good he is and how he performed. If you are in a relationship with him he will call you names and tell you that he is the alpha male - the dominant one. He can be very violent and have a very short temper. He really does lack self-confidence as he is desperately trying to live up to his ego, and he cannot bear being criticised and wants self-approval. He is the physical bully. Be careful as he can be very dangerous if tormented.

Mrs Defensive

This type of bully will use words and arguments to try and dominate you. She can use words and gossip to make your life hell. If you say anything Mrs Defensive will say something and it will always be the opposite to what you are saying. Sometimes Mrs Defensive will argue for the sake of arguing and will even forget what the argument was about. She does not have very good conversational skills and is not a very good listener. She continually talks about other people. She is draining to be around and constantly whinges and criticises everything and everyone. Mrs Defensive is an emotional person who will tell you what they think straight to your face. She is the verbal bully and with the right training can be handled easily. Mrs Defensive is so predictable.

Mr Dishonest

This type of bully will fabricate situations and stories to try to make himself look and feel superior. He will tell thousands of lies and will seem convincing. To be a good liar you have to have a good memory. The liar lives an illusion and really believes that he is something very special. He will lie about almost everything. He will gossip about you and spread rumours about your private life. He does this to break up your friendships and relationships with others. He is secretly very jealous. He will lie and make up secrets about you so that other people become interested in what he has to say. He will attack your character and criticise everything you do. They simply don't like you. The rumours he spreads are intended to hurt you, and he wants others to believe what was said is true Mr Dishonest is the psychological bully.

Mrs Devious

Mrs Devious is really hard to spot as she appears to be so nice and gentle. She becomes your best friend and in the beginning will seem to be very interested in what you have to say. Mrs Devious is learning about your strengths and weaknesses and will use this information as ammunition to conspire against you. She is very clever, witty and socially skilled. Mrs Devious talks calmly and uses her charm to work around you. She will put you down ever so slightly and her body language will appear to be supportive and gentle. She is difficult to spot as her body language does not reinforce the words and silences she uses. You may become confused and believe that you are being paranoid because her dominance is very subtle. Mrs Devious makes you question yourself and will create doubt in your mind, and it is this doubt that will play with your emotions. Mrs Devious is the emotional bully.

The Web Of Bullying

Joining the police service can be compared to joining a big family. The beat I work on has had the community bobby walk its street for generations. In fact the old fashioned constable is still talked about in pubs, community halls and schools each day. When I joined the service I was passed the reigns from a team of constables who had worked the same beat for 20 years. I meet the elderly community on a frequent basis and they still talk about "Copper James". On a summer's day I was walking the beat and I was stopped by a local retired police constable. We got chatting about the service and the people. I was amazed by his knowledge and experience. The stories started to flow and he asked me about certain families within the community. In that hour of talking to him I understood the background of the criminals on my patch. His story was compassionate as he really understood the people. It became apparent that he was talking to me about three generations of family problems. I was dealing with the grandchildren of both a bullying victim and a perpetrator. His story echoed the same issues that I was seeing on a weekly basis. It has not changed that much but just rolled from one generation to the next. Bullying is a learnt behaviour that is passed on from generation to generation. I have seen the institutionalised aspect of bullying almost too often, and its nature crosses all generations. Here are some examples.

Head teacher: "These children need the fear of god put into them, a good shake and a sharp shock."

Parent: "See that police man? He will take you away and lock you up, unless you behave."

Male abuser: "I don't hit my Mrs. If I have a problem with a man, I smash him."

Councillor: "I want to see a curfew at 9pm. If the children are on the street, they should be arrested".

Teenager: "Happy slapping, it's just good fun and a good laugh."

I see on a daily basis a great deal of unhappiness. Police work is very varied across all communities, but it is undeniable that 90 percent of police incidents involve bullying. Bullying is a state of mind that is why it is hard to see.

What Can I Do About Bullying?

The advice within this book will help you and give you the tools to prevent further bullying. You must tell someone that you are being bullied. If the person you tell does not listen then tell someone else and keep on telling until you are heard. Plan to tell someone you can trust because you don't want your feelings going back to the bully. As human beings we sometimes feel that we need to impose control but control can never be at the expense of someone else's happiness. Our motivation has to be a true, good intention that wishes to benefit everyone.

CHAPTER 2

DOMESTIC ABUSE

When someone is married or living with their bully, the method of abuse becomes more complex. Every aspect of your life can become controlled and dominated. Identifying with the bigger picture and putting these patterns of control together helps you identify that it is actually happening to you. It's not just in your head and you are not being paranoid. You are actually being targeted. It is sometimes truly amazing how another human being can make us believe that we are worthless. In many of the descriptions I have used I have focussed on the man being the aggressor. Bullying is not a battle between the sexes and both men and women exhibit such behaviours.

How They Control You

It is like living with a permanent sergeant major - you do as you're told. He will monitor all your daily activities and comment on how bad they were. He will snoop on you or block your telephone calls. He will tell you where you can and cannot go and prevent you from seeing friends and relatives. He may lock you in a room in the house and tell you when you are allowed out. Wherever you go he will follow you. He will check up on you and not allow you any time to yourself.

How They Dominate You

If you dare to challenge him he will pull out every stop to try and manipulate you. He will sulk and will make you submit to certain sanctions. These include; threatening to withhold money, stopping you from enjoying yourself, taking the car away, taking the children away, etc. He will play the wounded soldier and fane illness. He will conjure up make belief dramas and tell you that he is only doing what he is doing for your own good. He will blackmail you emotionally, such as threatening suicide and tell many lies. He will treat you like an animal and bark orders at you. He will not call you by your name. You are an object in his eyes. He will put you down persistently in front of other people. He will not listen to you as you are beneath him. He is not equal and will not help with childcare or housework.

How They Undermine You

He will tell many lies and keep important information close to his chest. Cleverly, he will make things more important than they really are. He will set and change the goal posts and you will never know if you are performing up to his standards. He will break promises and then blame you for his mistakes.

What Makes A Good Relationship?

We sometimes look at a relationship in terms of how we will benefit from it. Our society loves to make comparisons and we use certain unconscious measures of success or happiness. For example a successful partner is one who has a good job, a nice car, a big house, lots of friends, power, position and fame. Our society pushes the perfect life. We really cannot get away from it; when we turn the television on, pick up a paper or use the internet. Perfection is something that we are all aiming to achieve. The problem with this form of success is simple - you want more. You aspire to have a bigger house, a bigger pay check, a faster car, a more beautiful partner. When we live a life that is constantly demanding we eventually burn out. When you get that new car, you want another one and so on and so forth. The more you want and desire the greater amount of problems that you may encounter.

When we are threatened within an abusive relationship we can sometimes feel a great sense of loss and fear. That fear can sometimes be very subconscious. So many people make decisions based on a fear that is meaningless. You may be able to identify with the following statements: "I can't leave the relationship", "What about our house in the country?" Or: "I earn less, I won't be able to have my current lifestyle", "What will my mother say? She put up with it for years", "Nobody would believe me", "The shame of it, surely this doesn't happen to religious people?", "We are respectable members of the community. What would people think?" Our sense of fear is really our inner resistance to change.

A good relationship has the following qualities: it is a relationship that is consistent and accepts the ups and downs of life.

No violence	=	passive and loving
No stealing	=	gives and supports the family
No lying	=	trustworthy
No cheating with others	=	committed and respectful
No breaking up relationships	=	supportive, tolerant and helpful
No spiteful actions	=	says sorry, does not hold grudges

Your confusion is mixed up with many feelings. The abuse in your personal life does not fit with the idea of relationship perfection. This confrontation of ideas causes confusion. I call this the Walt Disney effect. Depending on your age you probably watched scores of Walt Disney movies. They always had happy endings and the prince always got his princess and they lived happily ever after. We are fed perfection from an early age and when we are confronted with the opposite of perfection we struggle immensely. We cling onto what it could be and how it should be. Unfortunately we are completely deluding ourselves and we live in the realms of make believe. It is so confusing living with a bully. After the violence he is just so nice. How could he do such things? We cling onto our idea of happiness and we accept him back. We tell ourselves, "He won't do it again, he will change". In an abusive relationship the reverse of the Walt Disney effect occurs. You are in such a degrading and unhealthy relationship that you do not know what normality really is. A good relationship is one that puts human qualities first. If you are lucky enough to have many comforts in life then that is a bonus. The first step to moving forward is simply accepting that you are being abused.

Sarah's Story

I met Ian four years ago. He was everything I looked for in a man. Good looking, strong, confident, sexy and successful. He was a real charmer. We started dating and he was an absolute gentleman. He would open the door for me. Ask me what I wanted and bought me clothes and gifts. He treated me like a princess and I was on cloud nine. Our relationship went from strength to strength. My family loved him and even my sisters were secretly jealous of me. Within months Ian asked me to marry him and we were walking down the aisle within twelve months. Our wedding was planned. I arrived in a Rolls Royce and walked down the aisle in absolute splendour. It was a wonderful day and everybody commented on how wonderful we were together.

After about six months of marriage I noticed that something was bothering Ian. He seemed really stressed at work. After a long hard day he would come home and start drinking. He said that he was stressed and I believed him. Ian started to demand more from me. He would come in from work and ask me, "Have you cleaned the house? Have you been shopping? What are you cooking me?" His behaviour started to change. He would check the house and see if I had cleaned properly. He would criticize my cooking and tell me that his mother could do better. He would tell me that it was my responsibility to look after him, to feed him, to cloth him, and to bath him. I just thought that he was stressed at work and put it down to that. We started to argue and Ian would behave in a very childish way. He would shout at me if I didn't agree with him. He would stare at me and smash his fist on the table. Socially Ian was always a great talker and everyone wanted to be around him. I noticed some really subtle changes. He would brag to our friends in front of me and tell them I was his woman and a woman's place was in the kitchen. He would slowly put me down and if I said anything or joined in with the conversation he would just ignore me. This made me feel really small and pathetic. Ian started to go out more regularly with his friends whilst I stayed home. He would come home late smelling of perfume. He always said that he thought that Sam, my school friend, fancied him. I would get really jealous and ask him what he was up to. Ian would laugh at me and tell me that I was being stupid and that he was just joking. I felt terrible. I confronted him about our relationship. I wasn't happy. Ian just walked up to me, screamed in my face and threw me on the floor. He stood over me and slapped me in the face. He said, "You deserve this. You made me do this." After this day Ian turned back into the old Ian. He bought me flowers. He arranged a candlelit meal for two and said sorry hundreds of times. I really believed him. I still loved him but somehow I knew in the depths of my heart something was not quite right. What could I do? I loved him but I could not go on like this."

What Should I Do?

Take a good look in the mirror and say to yourself, "I am not imagining things. This is really happening to me". Acceptance is the first stage to recovery. After the shock has sunk in, and you have acknowledged your distressing set of circumstances, you must tell someone. Believe it or not, so many people living around you know already what is happening in your life. Many people have experienced domestic abuse. You are not alone and will never be.

You and your children's safety are most important. You could do the following:

- Don't drink alcohol together – you always end up fighting.
- If he is going drinking all day with the lads stay with a family member.
- Pack a getaway suitcase and include all the family essentials: money, passports, birth certificates, cheque book, bank cards, identification, keys for your house, keys for work, legal documents, prescription drugs, clothing, benefit books and your driving licence.
- Teach your children to call 999 in an emergency.
- Consider purchasing a Howsar quick lock. This handy lock will give you time to get away. The portable lock allows you to lock a door in a short amount of time. Employ a diversionary tactic first "I am putting some make up on or I am getting you a beer from the fridge". Lock the escape door and get out of the house.
- Don't stay and face the violence. Seek help from a friend or neighbour, and get the children out of the house.
- Keep your mobile on you at all times and make sure it has sufficient credit.

- Add in your mobile phone a list of useful telephone numbers e.g. solicitor, doctor, crisis centre, etc. Put these contacts under your friends' names.
- If he is becoming aggressive then stay away from the kitchen and garage. There are many implements that could be used as weapons and cause serious injury.
- Don't go upstairs because many women are thrown down them. Avoid places where you could be trapped as he may lock you inside.
- If you have fixed appointments that your partner is aware of then change the time and location.
- Inform the children's school and make them aware that there may be trouble. Advise them that only you or another trustworthy person will pick them up.
- If you need to contact your ex-partner dial 141 before making your call as this will make it untraceable.
- Talk to your children. Tell them that they matter most and ask them not to tell others where you are living.
- Change your mobile phone; mobile phones can be "tracked" when they are switched on.
- Call the police. They will protect you. They can install free panic alarms and will actively support your case.
- Find the details of your nearest sheltered accommodation or crisis centre.

Only you know what to do and only you can make the right decision. It has to come from within. However, there are many issues that you need to consider and rushing into a decision will only unsettle you. When we are faced with life choices we have to make decisions that may alter the course of our life. Altering our life means that we have to change and as human beings change can be very uncomfortable. Life is change. It is that simple.

I always ask people the same questions. Do you want to be happy? Does your current lifestyle ensure that you and your family are totally happy? Answer these questions with absolute honesty and go with your gut feeling. So many people will tell you what to do. They will say, "I wouldn't put up with that. Just leave him. It's easy!" Your friends are not you. Once you have answered for yourself you have to be prepared to make one of two decisions. You can leave the relationship or you can stay.

Staying In The Relationship

It is no use staying in a relationship that has no firm foundation. For your relationship to be harmonious both of you have to be committed to change. There may be many aspects of your relationship that you may need to explore including your own inner thoughts and feelings. Both of you should be extremely proud that you have endeavoured to improve yourselves. There are many people who can help and support you. Consider advice from marriage guidance, family counsellors, debt advisers, substance misuse counsellors, anger management advisers, education, communication specialists, mediators, spiritual advisers, etc. It is important to seek advice from independent persons so that you will gain a clearer more balanced perspective.

Leaving The Relationship

Take a deep breath and be prepared for change. Take every day as it comes and do not plan too far ahead. It is hard but it will be worth it in the end. There are so many people who can support you and want to support you. There are many agencies that are there solely for you. Contact Women's Aid or Refuge and ask to be referred to a support worker. This person has a wealth of experience and will be able to advise you about your current rights and entitlements.

What Decisions Will I Have To Make?

Housing

Where are you going to live?

Could you stay with family or friends?

Would you move into a secure local refuge?

Employment

What are your rights and entitlements?

Can you afford to reduce your hours?

How can you gain new skills?

Benefits

What benefits are you entitled too?

Where do you go and how do you apply?

Finances

How much money do you have saved?

How do you share your savings?

What are your pension rights?

How do you come to a financial arrangement amicably?

Children

What do the children want?

How often do they want to see your ex-partner?

Do your partner's parents help with childcare?

Legal

What advice have you sought?

Support

How are you eating?

How is your health?

What are you doing to make yourself feel better?

What support groups are there?

Bullied

Miscellaneous

Do you need to learn new skills?

Who can you delegate too?

Who will support you?

What happens if . . . ?

Keeping Your Sanity

It is not your fault; it is always the bully's problem. You have been extremely brave. You have tried, you have adapted, and you have loved and forgiven. After all your efforts you cannot change him. Asking for relationship help is not a failure. Failure is not asking.

Never trick yourself into believing that all these decisions are excuses for not making the right decision. It is going to be a difficult time, but it will not last forever. Be comforted in the knowledge that you have made a decision that will affect generations of your family, ensuring that you are happier and contented. Talk to professionals and keep your story for compassionate people who are good listeners.

The search for true happiness - Sarah's Story

I suppose that I was tricking myself into believing I could be happy. We would discuss what we thought was going wrong and then we would do something about it. My partner came home one day and said that it was our financial debts causing all his stress and anger. I decided to work longer hours and make more money. It worked for a while, and we were happier.

As time went on we saw less of the children and things became increasingly tense. He blamed me for not doing the cooking, cleaning and looking after the children. I felt guilty because I was trying my best to be the perfect mother and to solve all our problems. We then decided to renovate the house and make it nicer. He said that if it was cleaner and more fashionable it would make us feel better. We spent weeks cleaning and renovating the house. It was really hard work, and at the end of it all we had a smarter space to live in.

It didn't change him. He was still moody and irritable. Then he said that our sex life needed to be spiced up. I agreed and we did all we could to make it more exciting. After a hard day's work I didn't feel like sex. It just made it worse. I suppose we were chasing happiness, and thought we could catch it and bottle it up. We would look at endless ways of avoiding the issue. We never talked but just action planned and dreamt about a new life. The abuse never stopped.

One day a good friend of mine pointed out to me where I was going wrong. She said that chasing happiness makes you even more miserable, and I thought to myself, "You're right". I examined the last year of my life. All I had done was make excuses. I worked longer hours in an attempt to please him, however, it brought me more pain and he threw it back at me and accused me of being a bad mother. I helped renovate our home. We increased our debts, worked harder and argued a lot. It wasn't really worth it. We tried to improve our sex life, but how could we? I was working all the hours and renovating the house. He yelled at me and told me that I was a useless lover. I couldn't win.

CHAPTER 3

HOW TO MINIMISE PHYSICAL CONFRONTATION

What Is Conflict?

Conflict is when we come into collision with someone and we have a disagreement about a particular problem. Bullying is different as the conflict is targeted at you. The stages of conflict can go unnoticed. They start from simple name calling, negative talk, accidental bumps, quarrels, arguments and then move onto violence. Behind a bully's mask a more sinister side can be hiding.

If left untreated bullying can develop into a violent confrontation. You can manage confrontational situations, but it is always better to avoid them in the first place. Each year people die from violence as a consequence of bullying. In the UK alone a women is killed every three days by a violent partner. In August 2008, 24 teenagers were killed as a result of knife crime. Workplace violence can occur and result in accidents and serious assaults. Violence is ugly, destructive and its use does not help anybody. It causes people to live in fear and destroys communities. Many professionals who deal with bullying may not want to advise you about confrontation. It is, however, a stark reality and will not go away. If you believe that your experience will not end up as a violent confrontation, you are simply burying your head in the sand. You do not know the motivation and mindset of your bully. Making an assumption could prove costly. The advice in this chapter will protect you and could save your life and that is why I have included it.

What is Street Awareness?

Street awareness is simply being alert to your surroundings, planning ahead and thinking about what is in front of you. You have to be prepared for a physical attack, and it is better to be prepared than pick up the pieces afterwards. You have to try and anticipate what your bully will do. Has he attacked other people before? Where did he attack them?

TRY THIS ONE
Write a story about your bully. Include what he does and how it makes you feel.

What Happens To Us When We Are Confronted With Violence?

When we are confronted with the threat of violence we can become scared or angry. You will notice many swirling feelings within your body. You may feel extremely nervous with butterflies in your stomach. Some people feel sick and paralysed with fear. All these feelings are **perfectly normal**. This is an aspect of fear called the fight or flight response. Evolution has prepared you for the threat of violence. Your prehistoric brain has developed a natural response to the threat of violence. Thousands of years ago our ancestors relied on this response daily. Our ancestors had to avoid predators and fight with warring tribes. Your body is preparing to run or fight.

Unfortunately the threat of violence is still with us today, however, it is small when we compare it to what our ancestors had to go through. Our brain transmits messages to the adrenal glands. These special glands release adrenaline. The hormone adrenaline is a special transmitter and travels around the body in an instant. It makes your heart beat quicker, your breathing rate increases, you become stronger and your tolerance to pain increases. Your reactions become faster and you can run and jump further. You are ready for action.

Sometimes when our bully torments us this natural reaction can have the reverse effect. You may become more agitated and stressed. Sometimes this can make the situation worse. If you feel yourself getting uptight and nervous take some deep breaths and say to yourself, "It is normal to feel like this." You will remain calmer.

Fear is only natural, as such try and control your anger and remain receptive to the events unfolding in front of you.

What Is Happening To The Bully Prior To Becoming Violent?

The bully at this point is going through a period of intense anger. The bully loses all mental control. His mind is making the situation worse. He is repeating and re-living all the anger in his mind. The bully is like a hamster in a wheel - he is going around and around, but not getting anywhere. However, if you remain calm in a confrontational situation you are in control. Being able to think is the key to diffusing conflict and avoiding violence.

How do I recognise the stages of confrontation?

<u>Situational Awareness</u>

Keep your head up and look around you. Every now and again look behind you. Gather information, and use your eyes and ears.

<u>The Stare</u>

The bully will hold his stare across the room, and is looking for someone to catch his gaze. At this stage the bully is secretly judging everyone and he is comparing weak victims with strong victims. This stage of awareness is an opportunity for you to avoid confrontation. Do not make it obvious but keep a watch over the bully.

<u>The Question</u>

If you have been indecisive and have not avoided the bully, you are ready for the next stage of confrontation. Your bully is going to project his feelings of inadequacy onto you and make you the problem. He will say, "HAVE YOU GOT A PROBLEM WITH ME?" What he is really saying is, "I am insecure, and I have a problem with you." Be aware that at this stage he has already planned to attack you. He may attack you verbally or physically depending on the circumstances.

The Body Language

His body language will change as the situation escalates. Even at the first stage look for the vital signs of body language that demonstrates violence. Communication is mostly through body language.

He will get closer to you. His chest will be inflated like a balloon, and his arms will puff outwards like a bird. He will stand tall and appear robotic. When he talks he will use his hands and point in a stabbing motion. His face will redden and his eyes will bulge, and his teeth may show. His jaw will tighten and he will appear bigger. He will constantly look around. He may stamp the floor.

The Provocation

Here it becomes increasingly tense. The bully will mutter words like, "Yeah, yeah, so, so." At this stage it will be almost impossible to communicate with them. What the bully is doing is target picking. He's looking at your body and deciding when and where he is going to attack you. The provocation can last some time depending on the bully. A violent bully will build up to this stage in a matter of split seconds. He will also swear at you.

The Attack

The distance between you and the bully will shorten and he may look for a sign of attacking opportunity, this will depend your own body language.

The majority of attackers are right-handed and right-footed. Do you know if your bully is right or left handed? In most cases your bully is going to throw a right hand hooking punch to the head. This isn't always the case as some like to grab and pull your hair.

In the case of workplace bullying: the bully may exhibit the first three stages of confrontation but may not necessarily move to violence. Employers sometimes call this behaviour "stress".

What Can I Do About It?

You cannot change a bully, only a bully can do that. You have to adapt to the bully's behaviour and make quick decisions.

<u>Situational Awareness</u>

Keep your head up and look around you, and every now and again look behind you. Gather information, and use your eyes and ears. Anticipate problems before they arise.

<u>The Stare</u>

It is absolutely normal to avoid confrontation and aggression. If you don't want to fight or argue, then **avoid the bully and leave the area**. There are many factors to consider at this stage. Is your bully in the company of others? Is he bigger and more aggressive than you? Has he been drinking alcohol? Does he have a history of violence? If your sixth sense starts to answer, "yes", to these questions, then do not try and be a hero and defend yourself just to make yourself look good. Swallow your pride and walk away. Prepare yourself. Do you have a panic alarm handy? Where is your defence spray? Where are you going to run? We some times call this tactical decision making or in everyday language "options".

<u>The Question</u> "HAVE YOU GOT A PROBLEM WITH ME?"

If your bully comes close, then step away, keep your hands up, and turn your palms outwards. Stand at a 45 degree angle, tuck your chin in and talk at a distance. Move side to side when talking to them. Say to them firmly "NO, I DON'T WANT TROUBLE. I DON'T WANT TO FIGHT." Don't turn your back on them and keep to the wall. Appear to give into them. Remember that by complying with their rules you are giving them a sense of control. You are also playing for time and preparing to respond.

The Body Language

Appear non-confrontational and keep your hands and palms facing outwards. This is a ploy as it tells the bully you are not willing to fight and gives them a sense of power. Tell them what they want to hear and keep on saying it even if it is, "I am sorry, I am sorry." Give them power.

Many women, who have been beaten by their partners, say sometimes it is best to say very little. By saying very little you do not add to the problem (in his mind). Every case is different and you will be the best person to decide.

The Provocation

Do not argue and try to remain calm. Keep well away from them. They are dangerous but you have options: you can run away, you can activate your panic alarm, spray them with defence spray, or you can attack.

The Attack

If you are getting attacked keep moving away from them. Cover your face and try and protect yourself. Do not let them get too close. Keep on shouting, "HELP, HELP, STOP, and STOP."

> **TRY THIS ONE**
> Find a busy city centre. Sit outside and enjoy a nice cup of coffee. Try and watch as many people as you can. Try and pick out Mr Angry and Mr Competitive. Watch how they walk and behave.

The Law And The Use Of Reasonable Force

The law in the UK allows you to defend yourself with reasonable force, which is force that is proportional to the threat that you are faced with. This is a subjective idea that depends on the individual circumstances. In basic terms if you are faced with one attacker, who is throwing punches at you, and you retaliate with a hard punch and you put your attacker to the floor, and then you run away, you are acting with reasonable force. If you stayed at the scene and continued to attack, you could be acting outside the law. Remember the law protects both of you and does not take sides. You can use reasonable force in the following circumstances:

The law allows you to attack your bully with a precautionary strike. If you are faced with violence and you are at the provocation stage, you could in effect trade blows before the bully attacks. If you are forced into this situation then attack and run. After the incident make sure you write down exactly what happened. Include the stages of violence and what your bully was doing. That way you will be able to evidence what happened and demonstrate why you acted as you did. This will save you a massive amount of aggravation if your bully reports the incident to the police.

The Use Of Defence Sprays -- A Safe Option

Stoppa Ltd has produced a legal defence spray that can be used in the UK. This spray is not an incapacitant like CS or Pepper spray. The spray works by impairing your bully's vision; if they can't see you they can't attack you. StoppaRed UV is a thick slimy goo designed to physically stick to an attacker giving you valuable time to react and escape. If you are threatened with immediate personal violence then this option is perfectly legal, but has to be reasonable and justifiable.

The 'goo' has a bright red colour to identify the attacker in the moments after an incident with added UV dye to help identify the attacker even days later. It is designed to be difficult to remove without running water. This spray can provide you with a chance to escape. It produces a very accurate stream over 3 metres for approximately 6 seconds or 6 one second bursts. StoppaRed UV has a maximum range of 4.5 metres.

This is a good preventative defensive spray that could be used in a variety of situations. Do not use the spray in windy conditions or crowded streets. The spray is best used at a distance and is not to be used in tight spaces.

Personal Attack Alarms are another device that you may consider using in a confrontational situation. They are best used in order to try and disorientate the bully. Place the alarm near the bully's face and shout as loud as you can. The bully will become disorientated and this should give you time to escape.

A Moral Dilemma

The decision to use force in a confrontational situation originates in the mind of the person who is being threatened. All decisions begin as intentions in our mind. Our values and beliefs shape who we are and will determine which decision we make. Different people hold differing attitudes to the use of violence or force. There seems to be a cultural shift to the use of "Non-Violence" in our society. This attitude of "Non-Violence" is encouraging, but I am afraid that its correct teaching in certain circumstances has been misinterpreted. Some educationalists are not teaching the real meaning of "Non-Violence". The real meaning of "Non Violence" incorporates spiritual values such as having no hatred for your bully, not retaliating with malice, not planning revenge, not holding a life long grudge, not being angered easily and showing the bully a form of forgiveness. I believe by not giving our children the correct explanation of "Non-Violence" we could in effect add to our children's suffering. A child who has been told not to defend oneself could be easily picked on and receive further injury. Our children need to understand that they must do all they can to reduce violence, however if they are in situation where they cannot run or summon help, they should be confident enough to use force as a method to protect themselves or their friends.

I have read in our news papers, angered parents who were told that the use of force was the wrong decision. This proves to me that educationalists are taking the meaning of "Non Violence" as a direct meaning and not looking into the deeper meaning of a Non-Violent Approach. If a child has been involved in a physical confrontation it is important to understand their decision making process. By understanding this process as a parent, guardian or teacher we will be in a better position to advise them about the correct understanding of Non-Violence.

I remember being at school and a certain bully terrorized the other children. The bully assaulted the other children and made our lives a misery. One day the bully tried to punch me at break time in the play ground. I had seconds to respond, I moved out of the way, I couldn't run as I was forced into a corner. My heart was racing and I was really scared. I had made my mind up and I used force to apprehend and dissuade the bully from assaulting me. My honest rational decision was based on a sense of compassion towards all my class mates. I severely disliked seeing them upset and hurt, I disliked the fact that they were being assaulted each and every day. I disliked the fact that we couldn't concentrate in class and achieve our potential. In these circumstances the use of force was based on the happiness of my fellow classmates. My sense of survival was strong. I didn't want to get hurt, I wanted to defend myself. My intention was not to injure the bully. In my mind I was practicing non-violence, but outwardly I was using force.

What Else Can I Do?

If you have been on the receiving end of a violent encounter or witnessed violence, it can affect you in many ways. Violence injures your body, mind and spirit and it can alter your perception of how the world really is. Continued abuse will grind you down until you adopt the view that the world is a horrible place, which is exactly what a bully wants you to believe. Remember for all the bullies in the world there are equally good people who benefit others, care for and support us.

I have interviewed many children in the presence of their parents. On many occasions the parent will take over and describe the effect that the bullying is having on them. Sometimes the parent will forget about the child and describe how it is affecting them. It is very common for the parent to be affected by the children's bullying. You may ask yourself, "Why?" Many parents have experienced exactly what their children are going through and start to relive the nightmare experiences that they have gone through. It is almost like a kind of post traumatic stress.

All too often I see the attitude of, "It's over, now get on with it." The reality is that it is not over. You have gone through a great deal of suffering and it is equally important that you deal with and manage your experience. There are many people who can support you, including family and friends. A trained counsellor will be able to guide you and help you make sense of it all. I strongly recommend that you seek this type of help. It will help you and your family in the long run. The last section in this book will guide you to the appropriate agency.

CHAPTER 4

PERSONAL SAFETY

You may fall into the trap of believing that you only have your own personal bully, and if the person stops bullying, then it will all go away. There are many situations where we may encounter a bully. Bullies are angry people and are sadly all around us. Statistically one in four women experience domestic abuse. One in four employees experience workplace bullying and the same applies to school related bullying. The reality is that we are all involved with, or have been a victim of bullying some time in our lives. Your safety is not just yours; it's shared with your family, friends and community. Many people care about you and want you to be safe. I have included many descriptions of personal safety; some may not be relevant at this stage in your life, however learning each section of advice will keep you and your family safe, now and for your future. Learning about personal safety can actively help others avoid such obvious problems.

Personal safety is useless if you do not plan ahead and try and anticipate your bully's plans. The bully wants to dominate and may potentially injure you. Human beings are remarkably robotic and thrive on routine. Your bully will identify your routine. He will know where you go and what you do. Once you have changed your routine, your bully may lose interest and change his victim.

TRY THIS ONE
Write down your weekly routine on a timetable, now record where your bully was and what they were doing. Identify times where you can avoid your bully.

The Danger Of Stubbornness

One of the main obstacles to maintaining your safety is your own attitude. If you are stubborn and adopt the attitude of, "Why should I?", then you are in real danger. A good friend of mine was being bullied by a work colleague. The bullying became worse and during a works night out it came to blows. My friend ignored the danger signs saying, "I've got my rights. I'm not leaving because of her.". She drank more alcohol and became increasingly stubborn. Her bully was more aggressive and larger than her; eventually my friend was attacked and ended up in hospital. She has a large scar on the side of her face and has been left traumatized by the attack. My friend chose to ignore the signs of confrontation and ended up worse off. A field mouse does not play by a hawk's nest, does it?

Avoiding Confrontation on the Street

Attacks by strangers in the street are still rare and account for a very small percentage of violent attacks. You are far more likely to be attacked by someone you know.

Be very careful if you witness others involved in an argument, especially couples walking home from a night out. Do not put your ego before your safety. We all know that it is wrong, but use your common sense. Sometimes doing the right thing can get you into real trouble. Many people have intervened and have come off worse. Stay back, observe and call the police.

You should think about how you would act in different situations before you are in them. Think about whether you would stay and defend yourself (using reasonable force), and risking further injury, or whether you would give an attacker what they want to avoid injury. There is nothing wrong with doing either, but you should think about the options, as there will be no time to do so if you are attacked.

Technology can help you stay safe, 3ARC limited have developed a number of safety products that allow you to contact help and support at the touch of a button. The 3ARC Angel system connects your mobile phone to a 24hr dedicated response service using a predefined 0871 number. When your body releases adrenaline fine motor skills become very difficult. The 3ARC system allows you to contact the control centre by speed dialling the number 3 on your mobile phone. Once you have made contact with the control centre your personal details and history will be shown to the operator. The operator will then be able to summon help from a variety of sources including family members, neighbours or the police.

3ARC also offer a GPS locating system know as Track and Talk. This system acts as a mobile phone, when you activate the handset the control operator will be able to speak to you and pin point your exact location. Your personal details will be accessed and the appropriate help will be notified. This technology could save you from immanent danger.

Consider the following advice:

- Keep to main routes and avoid places of darkness. Stick to well lit and busy areas. Plan your route and stick to areas where there is CCTV. The more people about the less likely you are to be attacked.
- Try and vary your times and locations when travelling. Often your bully will be waiting for you.
- Try to look and act confident. Look like you know where you are going and walk tall.
- You might like to spread your valuables around your body. For example keep your phone in your bag, your house keys in your trouser pocket and your money in your jacket.
- When travelling, make sure you are with a friend and tell someone where you are going.
- When you leave your home, tell someone where you are going, when you will be returning and how you can be contacted. Leave a timetable of your likely whereabouts with loved ones.
- Carry a mobile phone and make sure it has enough credit on it.
- Avoid late nights, and avoid the peak times when people are drunk, typically on weekends between 9 pm and 2 am. Your bully is more dangerous when under the influence of drink or drugs.
- You can use reasonable force in self-defence. You are allowed to protect yourself with something you are carrying (for example, keys or a can of deodorant). You could carry the Stoppa Defensive Spray. This spray is legal to carry and could prevent an attack from occurring, giving you vital seconds to run away.

- Shout 'fire' rather than 'help' as it can get more results.
- Try and use the mirrors of cars and reflections of shop windows -- that way you can see what is behind you.
- When out walking, you should avoid using your mobile phone or texting on the go. This distraction can stop you from being aware of your surroundings. Similarly listening to your iPod whilst walking can limit your awareness.
- Do not get drunk, you will not be able to think clearly and act decisively.
- Avoid dark gloomy places, subways, bridges, open fields and dark lanes. Never take a short cut.

Consider What You Are Wearing And What You Are Carrying

Depending on the social occasion, consider what type of clothing could be a hindrance. Avoid poor foot wear; you can't run with flip flops or high heels. Avoid wearing hoodies and large anoraks, as they may block your peripheral vision and can easily be used to stop you seeing. Jewellery can be used to strangle, and (expensive) earrings can easily be ripped out of your skin and can cause injury. Long hair can be used as a tool to grapple with, so tie it up. Keep expensive personal items to a minimum; do you really need your iPod, camera, mobile, laptop, etc? When carrying a rucksack, carry it on one shoulder, so that if you sense there may be trouble, dump it and run. Consider wearing sunglasses in the daytime, that way you can avoid eye contact and check out what is going on.

Public Transport

Public transport can be a daunting experience and has its dangers. Plan well ahead and ask yourself whether you really need to travel. When you enter the carriage have a good look around. Can you smell alcohol? Does anybody grab your attention? Sit near other people; the driver if you are on a bus or near the conductor if you are on a train. Move if someone makes you feel uncomfortable.

Driving

- Keep your car in good condition and try not to run out of petrol
- Try to park in well lit or busy areas, and if you park during the day think about what the area will feel like after dark
- If you break down on the motorway follow the arrows to the nearest phone. Do not cross the carriageway. wait outside your car (as far away as possible from the carriageway) unless you feel threatened, in which case you should sit in the passenger seat
- Lock the car's doors when you get into the vehicle
- Use your electronic key fob in the correct way. if you press the key once it will only open the driver's door
- Do not give lifts to or accept lifts from people you do not know, or do not know very well.

Taxis

- If you are going to be out late or don't want to travel on public transport on your own, try to arrange a lift home with someone you know or make your journey by taxi
- Get to know your local driver, and take his/her personal mobile number, that way you can ring them if you need help
- You should always ensure that you travel in a licensed taxi by checking the vehicle's signage or plate and the driver's badge; you should never agree to travel in an unlicensed vehicle with an unlicensed driver
- If you pre-book your taxi make a note of the company you are using, and the telephone number, and if possible leave it with a friend
- When you get to your destination ask the driver to wait until you are inside

- If travelling alone always sit behind the driver in the back seat
- If you feel uneasy ask to be let out in a well-lit area where there are plenty of people
- If in any doubt make an excuse and don't get in the vehicle.

Personal Information and Cyber Bullying

Personal information is information that you give freely about yourself on a website, social networks, emails, text messages and chat rooms. There are many positives to this way of communication; it is cheap, fast and effective. However, there are many downsides and this new age of communication can make bullying worse. You have to decide which method of communication best suits you and weigh up the pros and cons.

The written word can be misinterpreted very easily. Communication is 80 percent non-verbal, as our body language, and tone of voice and presence give a true indication of what we are really saying. What we are truly saying in our message depends on how well the person listens. The ability to listen is a very important skill; it is not just about the spoken word it is also about feelings. The person doing the listening will listen better if he is feeling calm and relaxed. Unfortunately text message, email and social networking do not truly allow us to communicate effectively.

Social Networking Sites, Email and Text Messages

Communicating this way can be very impersonal as your audience cannot understand how you are feeling. A bully can pass all sorts of information on the web about you, and a hate campaign can form.

- Don’t put your personal email, mobile telephone number or address on the site
- Don’t give people ammunition and tell the whole world what you like and dislike; your bully will have an even stronger advantage
- Don’t just add friends just for the sake of it

- If you are receiving threatening text messages from your bully then store them on your phone; if it continues and you receive further hoax calls, change your number
- Store and save threatening emails
- Withdraw from an abusive site
- Do not respond to threatening messages; do not take the bait.

At School

- Avoid places where there are no teachers or adults
- Take refuge in the school library
- Arrange to be picked up by an adult
- Ask to go to the toilet during lesson time
- Consider purchasing a Howsar quick lock. This handy lock will give you time to get away. The portable lock allows you to lock a door in a short amount of time.
- Look around to see what is happening; look behind you.

Workplace Bullying

- Have a good look at the hazards in your workplace; you don't want to get involved in a confrontational situation next to a scalding kettle or next to some heavy machinery
- Look after your own and others' welfare; your colleagues will support you and will thank you for your co-operation
- Avoid lone working; you are making your self a target
- Avoid works parties; many people can get sucked into forming cliques and enemies over petty issues
- Research company policies and your statutory rights.

All the personal safety advice given is tried and tested and is based on experience. Some of the advice may seem precautionary and not applicable to your situation, but circumstances change. Anybody can be a victim of bullying or a victim of crime.

CHAPTER 5

HOW TO DEAL WITH VERBAL BULLYING

You must remember the old saying, "Sticks and stones will break my bones, but names will never hurt me". So why do words hurt so much and, how do we minimise those hurtful words?

To understand what a word is we first have to understand what an emotion is. Emotions and feelings are the same thing. You can't touch them. You can't see them. They are hard to describe, but you can definitely feel them. The clue is in the word e-motion. Motion means to move and that is exactly what your emotions do. Close your eyes and think of a time when someone made you really mad. Try and relive that moment. Imagine what you were feeling and concentrate on the feeling of anger.

Does the following description bear some reality? I feel crazy, fiery, bursting, red hot, tense, agitated, and aggressive. What we are really describing is an inner vibration. Certain emotions vibrate more than others and move us to act in certain ways. Think of emotions as constructive or destructive. Anger is a destructive emotion. It causes more problems, blocks understanding and leads to frustration. Compassion is a constructive emotion it aids communication, builds trust and helps you.

Words start from the inner level of someone who is speaking. They begin as vibrating emotions; when the person talks his voice box changes those vibrations into sounds. Sound at the scientific level is a series of waves and waves are oscillating vibrations. When a bully uses harsh words with real intent behind them, it really sends a clear message. What is happening is that those words communicate on an emotional level because those words invoke a greater level of vibration within you. The greater the inner vibration of a word, the more harmful it is.

When somebody says, "They are only words. Ignore it", they are really saying, "I don't want to help." Words and the associated emotion behind their meaning are very destructive. In order to prevent words from piercing our armour, we first have to understand our emotions. The word "understand" literally means to stand under something. If you analyse and stand under something you look at it in a different light. Once we understand our emotions we are in a better position to work with them and cool them down. We have the choice not to be affected by the bully's harsh words. The bully does not have a choice because he continues to react to his emotions and makes the same mistakes. The poor bully! You will become flexible and stronger.

We are taught to communicate with words, but words conceal our thoughts, beliefs and emotions. In order for you to understand the real meaning behind words you have to listen in a different way. Listen with your eyes; what is the person's body language saying? Listen with your heart; how are you feeling? Listen with your mind; what do the words mean? Listen with your intellect; what are you going to do? When you consider the person's message from this aspect you truly begin to understand the correct message. By applying this technique you are in a better position to gauge if the bully really means what he is saying or if it is simply just hot air.

What Does The Bully Say?

The bully will use words that are reflective of his feelings. If he is feeling really angry he will use short, sharp and easy words. These words are blunt and direct: "You bas**rd", "You fat bitch".

The bully, if more socially skilled, will mix up words that are designed to play on your mind. He will use silent put downs, jokes and banter. One of the most obvious tactics is the character assassination. The bully will describe and label a person's weaknesses, implying that you have the same attributes. The bully will make references to other people, but secretly they are targeting you. "I don't like Jayne, she's always moaning. Fat people are lazy, aren't they?"

How Do I Minimise The Effect Of Hurtful Words?

You have to remain calm, take a breath, and try to relax. You know what is coming as it is all so predictable.

Water Of A Duck's Back

This is a technique that reduces verbal bullying and it can reduce insults from escalating. Fogging, as it is traditionally known, involves agreeing with insults as far as practicably reasonable. You are in control and you reduce the chances of violence. You have to adopt a firm stance and appear confident. Practice this technique in the mirror, and watch your body language. Stand tall, open your arms outwards, and look at your bully. Try and rehearse in your mind what you are going to say. Imagine saying the words with confidence. When you are insulted adopt the following sayings and believe them: "That's true", "that might be true", "I can see why you think that's true", "that's your opinion".

This technique reinforces the bully's petty rule book; you haven't broken his rules and therefore are not annoying him. It is difficult to do because you may feel that what you are doing is wrong. You have every right to feel aggrieved, however, your actions are successfully managing his behaviour and making the best of a situation. Adopt this technique until you have enough time to get away from the bully.

By agreeing you are not giving the bully more ammunition and you are not giving them an opportunity to increase their dominance.

The Dead End

Bullies will often communicate indirectly when looking to criticize you. They will do this by asking questions. The questions are designed to make you consider yourself. It is not very nice when someone continually asks questions. You can feel like you are on trial. In order to turn a situation around and reverse a situation, you have to ask the bully a question and get him to make a statement. Once he has made a statement and you understand his point of view, you can then adopt a fogging response. You may have seen this technique employed previously -- politicians are expert at it.

The Blame Game

When we are verbally battling with our bully we can unwittingly involve ourselves in the blame game. I have seen this response in countless situations: outside nightclubs, in homes, at parties and in the school yard. In the majority of the situations it ends up as an escalation of violence. If you feel that you are getting pulled into the blame game, step back and remain calm.

Blame is about finding fault with a person and not being able to agree about a solution to a particular problem. On the face of it you may see two people arguing about a problem, but look deeper and ask yourself the question why? If we go back to the very start of this book, and remind ourselves why people bully, we will understand blame a little bit better. When we hold onto our opinions tightly we grab onto them, as if they matter at the cost of our lives. We defend our view because we believe that we are always right. We hold these ideas close to our hearts and they become real. When we blame we always find fault with the other person as we cannot see our faults from a different perspective. When two conflicting people hold strong ideas they naturally conflict. In order to manage the blame situation you have three options:

1. You could walk away and move on, realising that your bully doesn't have the capacity to communicate as a decent human being.

2. You could overpower your bully, although this isn't the wisest thing to do, as you then become the bully.

3. You could alter your communication style and co-operate with the bully. Two magnets of the same polarity always repel. If you turn one magnet around, they stick together and become one. In the same way with the magnets, you have to merge with the opposing magnet and the only way to do this is to co-operate.

Every Saturday you can witness this effect for free by going to your local sports ground. It happens in sport all the time. No matter what the situation, sport, relationships, work or play, you will see this pattern form.

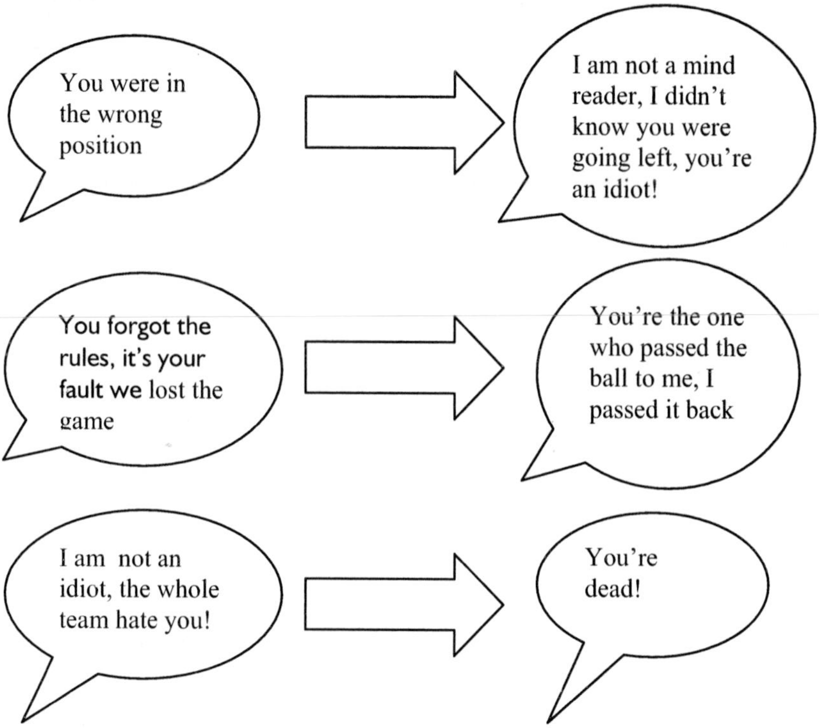

TRY THIS ONE

When your bully starts to argue look beyond the words he uses. Try to visualise his insecurities. The more he argues the greater his insecurities. You may start to develop some compassion for your bully. He is probably suffering from greater unhappiness than you are.

I saw you looking at him.
That's true. I thought I recognised him.

You've probably have had sex with him -- you dirty bitch.
That's your opinion.

Well have you?
You think that's true, but I really love you and no one else.

You have dirty ginger hair.
That's true, I have ginger hair.

Gingers smell
and are ugly.
That's your
opinion.

You're ugly.
I can see why you
think that's true.

She's such a bullshitter.
That's your opinion.

What do you think about fat Diane?
I can see why you are thinking those things.

The secret to co-operating with people is the style in which you communicate. A good communicator will adapt the talking strategy to the level at which the bully understands. Power is a key component in the conversation. A simple way to think about this is to categorise your bully into the communicator in the role of either a parent, adult or child. If I said to you in the voice of a strict parent, "GO TO YOUR ROOM AND CLEAN IT!", and you responded in the voice of a child, "I AM ALWAYS CLEANING MY ROOM!", the probability of the conversation ending in an argument is high. In terms of the bullying situation your aim is to try and get the bully to communicate as an ADULT. The only way to do this is to consider how your bully is communicating and adapt your style. By adapting your style to suit the bully you lessen the chances of verbal bullying.

Blaming someone is a poor way of communicating. When we focus on a person's faults they react by becoming even more defensive; you react by increasing your personal pressure. The whole situation escalates out of control. People enjoy talking about themselves and relax a little when they can tell you about themselves. The bully is no exception, and he loves to be in control. To try to avoid blaming, you have to ask open questions. Open questions start with: who. what. why, where, when, and how.

If you ask the bully a range of questions you get to understand him better. He gets his feeling. and emotions off his chest and you begin to build bridges. When people are under stress and in conflict they tend to mix up their opinions. An opinion is a mixture of fact and feelings. A fact is what actually happened in time and space. Sometimes we muddle up our own view with our facts and feelings, because of this muddling and conflict we then blame others.

Because we communicate in a way that includes fact and feelings it is better to ask questions about fact and feeling. For example ask yourself; "What happened?", "How do you feel about that?", "Why do you feel that way?".

Start with yourself, and understand your own feelings.

Putting It All Together:

Stay Calm

Count to ten and breathe deeply. Remind yourself that how you react to the situation will have an effect on a peaceful outcome. Say very little.

Work Out Your Point of View

Ask yourself some questions;. "How are you feeling?", "What has happened?". Try to make sense of your point of view.

Explain Your Point Of View

Avoid blaming the bully.

Explore Your Point Of View

Ask the bully the same questions. Tell them that you are listening and want to understand them.

Problem Solve

Agree to co-operate and compromise. If you have tried all means to achieve a resolution and it does not work, then forgive, avoid and move on.

At Home

The process of exploring and communicating in a relationship will take time. Set yourself time in the day, away from the children and work it out together. Do not argue in front of the children. Be gentle with each other and do not take it too seriously. With constant practice you will begin to communicate in this way naturally.

At Work

By improving your communication style you will achieve more and become more competent. This style of communication shows composure, maturity and level-headedness. This level of composure actually calms people down in stressful situations.

CHAPTER 6

HOW TO DEAL WITH YOUR EMOTIONS

Bullying plays havoc with our emotions and that is why it hurts so much when we experience such unnecessary abuse. It is difficult to come to terms with why someone can be so cruel. Bullying does not make sense and that is why it can be difficult to understand.

What Are Your Emotions?

Our emotions are related to our sense of identity or our "I". A person who holds strongly onto an imaginary sense of self importance will generally struggle with emotions and mental anguish. If I hold myself in high esteem my level of anger will increase. However, if my approach is flexible the same situation would appear different. For example, if I had just spent thousands of pounds on a number of beauty treatments and I held the belief that I was now more beautiful and attractive, and you came to my home and you did not comment on my fabulous looks, I would feel pretty miserable. This form of mental pain is related to my inner feeling of self importance. I hold my beauty as supremely important. However in the same set of circumstances if I reduced the importance of looking good in my mind, and you again failed to comment on my fabulous looks then my sense of mental pain or defensiveness would actually reduce. Emotions begin in the mind.

How Do I Recognise My Emotions?

Emotions cannot be scientifically measured. However, scientists can measure the effect of emotions by measuring their effect on the body. For example fear can increase your heart rate, adrenaline or blood pressure. The only scientific tool that has been developed to measure real emotions is called the "human being". You can do it easily, all you need to do is find a quiet place, sit and relax. If you have had a hard day sit down and find a breathing space for 15 minutes. If you have decided that you are angry, breath deeply and concentrate on the inner feeling. Re-visit the experiences that made you feel angry and hold the feeling of anger in your mind. In your mind compare the feeling of anger with the "tick-tock" of an old-fashioned alarm clock. Give the emotion of anger a numerical value. Breathe deeply, inhaling for four seconds and exhaling for four seconds. Visualise with time; the alarm clock slowing and the inner vibration easing.

When we learn to play a musical instrument we attribute a particular sound or vibration with a particular note. A skilled musician will be able to listen to the sound and tell you what the note is. In the same way feelings (inner vibrations) become the sounds and you become the musician. You can now give each emotion a name and recognise how it feels and its qualities.

This very simple exercise allows you to tune in with how you are feeling. I have seen thousands of people in distress over the years. When people are in distress they find it difficult to communicate their feelings. Emotions are generally described using words and this is where we fall down. Emotions are not words. There are many benefits to learning about our emotions. When you are able to recognise a harmful emotion you are in a better position to apply positive thoughts in order to stop the emotion from developing. You will be in a better position to walk away from an escalating situation and show restraint and composure. By following this advice you would have decreased the chances of being attacked or injured.

What Emotions Will I Be Feeling?

The Emotion of Humiliation - disgraced, defeated, alienated

When you have been humiliated you feel like you want to crawl into a cave and disappear. Humiliation means to inform other people about your weaknesses or faults and broadcast those facts to many people. The effect is of a silent paranoia or public hysteria. Your ego takes a battering and you feel very small indeed. It can be a very powerful tool if used against someone in a bullying situation.

The Opposite of Humiliation - confident, self-assured

Focus on the feeling of humiliation for ten minutes in a quiet room. Visualise the feeling of humiliation vibrating inside your heart. How fast does the feeling vibrate? Give this emotion a number.

The Emotion of Anger - mad, bitter, irritated, resentful

When you feel angry you lose present control and can act in many different ways. Anger is a turbulent thunderous mind that wants to explode.

The Opposite of Anger - loving, friendly, peaceful, agreeable

The Emotion of Fear – scared, frightened, worried, nervous

When you feel fearful you are worried that you may come to some harm. Fear can be in the physical sense in that you are concerned that you may be injured. Psychological fear is a fear that your status or identity may be threatened.

The Opposite of Fear - confident, trusting, hopeful

The Emotion of Hurt - distress, upset, tearful, sad

When we are hurt by someone we feel that our ideas were not listened to and that our opinions do not count. We value our personal contribution and like to feel valued and part of the team. Hurt is a feeling that we can make worse by constantly reminding ourselves of the hurtful situations that we have encountered in the past.

The Opposite of Hurt – relieved, comforted, cheerful, glad

The Emotion of Disgust – repelled, put off by

When we are disgusted, we feel that avoidance is the only answer. Not only do we feel that we want to avoid, but disgust leaves a lingering and lasting bad feeling towards another.

The Opposite of Disgust – affectionate, fond of, impressed

TRY THIS ONE

Sit down in a quiet room and relax. Try and relive the feeling of fear. Now try and relive the feeling of trust. Which emotion makes you feel good inside? Which emotion do you want to move to?

> **TRY THIS ONE**
> If you adopt the same exercise with each descriptive emotion you will quickly be able to identify with your emotions. This takes time and effort. However, you will be able to signal a deep level of understanding.

What Can I Do To Make Myself Feel Better?

The bully torments you because his actions are a reflection of how he is feeling. If he feels angry he will act with anger and resentment. The bully transfers his negativity on to you. You will then feel negative and upset. When you are ill you take medicine in order to feel better. The medicine has the opposite effect and neutralises the illness. The practice of meditation acts like medicine. With the power of thought you can counteract the effect of negative emotions.

If our mind is peaceful we will be free from worries and mental discomfort and so we will experience true happiness and relaxation. But if our mind is not peaceful we will find it very difficult to be happy and relaxed. Bullying destroys our peace and happiness. However, it is only you who can decide to make things better.

What Is Meditation?

Meditation is the practice of focussing your mind on a positive, virtuous feeling. For example if you are feeling bitter and resentful and you focus your meditation on the feeling of love. After spending time concentrating on the feeling of love, your mind will feel more peaceful. Meditation has its origins in many of the world's religions. It is a technique and there is not a right way or wrong way to meditate. The goal of meditation is to train the mind to think more positively. If we train in meditation, our mind will gradually become more and more peaceful, and we shall experience a purer form of happiness. Eventually we shall be able to stay happy all the time, even in the most difficult circumstances.

What Are The Benefits Of Meditation?

Meditation has been scrutinized by many scientific studies. It has been proven that the technique of meditation can reduce stress and improve relaxation.

How Do I Meditate?

Meditate in a clear and quiet place.

Do not rush straight into the meditation but spend a few moments to relax into a comfortable posture with your back straight but not tense.

Always begin by developing a positive wish to benefit yourself and others through your meditation.

Try not to forget the objective meditation. The objective is the type of feeling you are trying to focus on.

Before you rise from meditation, mentally dedicate the positive energy that you have created to yourself and others.

Throughout the day try and recall the feeling of meditation as often as you can. Use it to guide everything you think, say and do. Spend twenty minutes each day meditating.

What Can I Expect?

The practice of meditation will take some time to master, and take each session slowly. Meditation is a skill that can be learnt. Like all skills you have to practice them daily. Do not be hard on yourself in the early days. You will get glimpses of a peaceful mind, however, with time and effort the experience of peace will lengthen.

An Actual Meditation – "Breathing Meditation"

Sit on a chair in quiet a room by yourself. Unplug the phone and give yourself twenty minutes of uninterrupted time. Keep your feet firmly on the floor. Place your hands in a cupped position and find a relaxed position with your back straight. Close your eyes. Take a deep breath and count in your head to the number four. Exhale with a long relaxed breath and count to the number six. Continue with this until you are feeling a little more relaxed. Spend five minutes breathing deeply.

Thoughts will keep whizzing into your head. Don't try and stop them but let them come and go. Thoughts are like the tide; they come in and go out. Try not to let the tide sweep you out to sea. Continue to focus on your breath. As you inhale feel the cool air pass your nostrils, and as you exhale feel the warm air pass through your nostrils. Focus on the feelings of cold air and warm air. Continue breathing deeply for six counts and exhaling for six counts. Try and hold your concentration for five minutes. Within this breathing meditation we are aiming to focus on the feeling air.

Relax and breathe. As you relax maintain your concentration. As you inhale imagine the breath as white smoke entering your body, helping you and nourishing every cell in your body. As you exhale imagine thick black smoke leaving your body, making you more rejuvenated and stronger. Imagine that you are slowly cleansing your mind. Visualise your pure heart and feel at peace with yourself.

Slowly resume by concentrating on your breath, enjoying that space of calm and happiness. Open your eyes."

A Meditation To Oppose Anger - Focussing And Harvesting A Loving Mind

"I feel really angry. My stomach is churning up inside and I feel really irritable. I just want to punch someone. How dare they do this to me? I hate them, and I hate my life. I just want to cry, Ahhhhh!"

Meditation

Sit on a chair in a quiet room by yourself. Unplug the phone and give yourself twenty minutes of uninterrupted time. Keep your feet firmly on the floor. Place your hands in a cupped position and find a relaxed position with your back straight. Close your eyes. Take a deep breath and count in your head to the number four. Exhale with a long relaxed breath and count to the number six. Continue with this until you are feeling a little more relaxed. Spend five minutes breathing deeply.

Today there are many people who exist to benefit you and do so to ensure all your happiness. Believe it or not, but kindness is all around us. Every act that a person does has at the heart of it an act of kindness or goodness. Starting with you, I want you to consider the kindness that you have received. As you read through the following descriptions I want you to think about your own life and feel each person's happiness.

The clothes you are wearing were the result of someone else's happiness. Many people were involved in making the clothes in harsher conditions than you are living in. Roads were built to help transport the clothes. The roads were built by hard physical work in very demanding circumstances. The labourers were working for their happiness and yours. Eventually the clothes were displayed in a shop. You were given money so that you could purchase them.

The room you are sitting in was constructed to provide your family with shelter and security. The architect, the builder, the carpenter, the plasterer all co-operated to provide you with this basic need. The meal you ate last passed through many hands before you ate it. The farmer, the packager, the cook all worked together to feed you. They did this to provide happiness to themselves and others.

Happiness is born out of love. The book you are reading was given to you as others want you to be happy. Your family spent hours teaching you to read and sent you to school. The teacher taught you many skills so that you can co-operate in this world. All your daily needs have been taken care off. Somebody somewhere has considered your problems and has provided a solution to your suffering. We have central heating, clean sanitation, medicines, charities, transportation, education, music, etc. All that is around us has been provided by many people. Indeed I have written this book as I genuinely want you to be happy.

Focus on feeling and understanding that others have acted as a result of love. As you visualise all this kindness focus on the feeling of love that is developing in your heart. Now keep and hold the feeling of love within your heart until it begins to fade away.

As it fades away remind yourself about how many people have benefited you and acted out of love, once again focus and concentrate on the feeling of love.

As you rise out of the meditation return to focussing on your breath, imagine all your anger slowly rising in the air as thick black smoke. As you take a breath imagine pure light entering every part of your body.

A Meditation To Heal Life's Problems

This powerful meditation is also know as "taking and giving". It is a meditation that heals and restores.

"I want you to imagine in your mind all the problems, anxieties and fears that you have about the bullying that you are experiencing. Picture the people, circumstances and situations clearly. Remind yourself about the hurt that you have been feeling and the emotions that have accumulated in your heavy heart. Now imagine rising above all this hurt and clearly seeing all that has happened to you. Slowly imagine turning these visions into thick black smoke. As you take a deep breath in, imagine all the black smoke entering your body. The smoke clears as it enters your heart and dissolves. Now as you exhale imagine sending rays of warm, pure light from your heart breaking all the unhappiness in the world. Send as much light to as many people as you can. Continue to use this visualisation as you breathe in and out. Focus your concentration on this meditation for as long as you can"

There are many forms of meditation. Meditation can be used to improve your mental happiness. Try different styles of meditation and experiment with the one that suits your particular needs. Some styles focus on a particular religious aspect and others do not. It is entirely up to you.

CHAPTER 7

SHIFTING PERSPECTIVE

Bullied

Being bullied or harassed can cause us a great deal of distress. Sometimes stress and worry can spiral out of control and we can add to that feeling of despair. We can create our own personal problems and walk around with a permanent grey cloud. We become unaware because we continually repeat the hurt and upset that we have been feeling. Our mind will focus on an upsetting event and constantly play the event over and over again. Imagine if you were made to watch a scary horror film -- how do you feel after you have watched the film? Imagine watching the film on ten occasions one after the other -- how would you feel? Repeating the hurt that you have received helps no one. You become more negative and people avoid you, and you become more frustrated and add to the problem.

The problem of repeating negative emotions such as anger, hatred, and mistrust is very serious. When we repeat the hurt we relive it and we make it look, feel and seem bigger. We have created a monster that does not actually exist. This is ironic, as the bully also repeats the same habit prior to abusing you. If you feel that this is happening to you, you need to take a break, re-assess and take a different perspective. The following ideas may help you. Make your own self care plan and keep it with you for life. If things are getting too much, revert back to your self care plan. Sometimes we do forget to look after ourselves, or don't know how to.

Use Visualization As A Coping Tool

When your bully is particularly nasty visualise them standing as a small clown with a big red nose. Use any type of visualization that helps you make light of a situation.

Focus On Something Else

Getting away from your troubles will allow you to reflect differently. The solution to life's troubles is sometimes right under our noses and focusing on something else helps us to see things differently.

Relax

Do not add to your busy life. A good old fashioned day off is just what the doctor ordered. Do the things that comfort you; take a nice hot bath, read a book, eat chocolate, or have a massage.

Do not Drink Alcohol

Alcohol is a depressant and will make you feel more depressed the next day. Using alcohol to solve your problems will inevitably lead to further feelings of despair.

Eat Regular Meals That Are Well Balanced And Contain The Correct Nutrients

Skipping meals adds to fatigue and stress. Certain foods are mood boosters.

Get A Good Night's Sleep

After a good night's sleep we begin the day in a better frame of mind. Try and keep to the same routine. Go to bed at 10 pm and rise at about 7 am.

Happiness List

Make a list of all the things that make you feel happy. Carry the list with you and read it once in a while. Focus on the feeling of happiness. Do the things that make you feel happy and treat yourself.

Help Others

Helping others helps you. By making someone else's life more pleasurable you gain friendship, support, skills, respect and new opportunities.

Have Fun

Be spontaneous and decide to do something new; push your boundaries and enjoy the moment.

Look After Your Pet

You do not have to own your own pet instead you could walk a neighbour's dog or go and help at the local cattery. Animals offer so much happiness.

Exercise

Exercise has been proven to lift your mood. You do not have to be super fit as 20 minutes a day is all you need to do. Start slowly and build yourself up. Exercise has to be fun otherwise you will not commit to getting fit.

Meet New People Or Start A New Hobby

The old saying "A change is as good as a rest" is certainly true. A new direction in life can offer new opportunities. Education is an attitude of mind and helps to broaden your experiences. Look in your local library or town hall. Research groups on the internet.

Play Music

Classical music works on different levels and has a soothing effect on your mind, body and soul. The power of music is astonishing.

Write Poetry

Writing poetry allows us to express our inner feelings and helps us make sense of our world.

Walk In The Country

The green pastures of the countryside relax and soothe us, and combining the elements with exercise will rejuvenate you. The peace and tranquillity of nature has a calming effect.

Visit Your Friends And Family

Being around the people who matter to us helps us to reaffirm who we are and what we stand for. Visiting the people who care for us gives us an opportunity to talk and express ourselves.

Start The Day With Meditation

Your perception of the world starts with you. Starting the day with a clear mind allows you to concentrate and listen clearer. Qualities such as patience, calmness and tolerance develop. By becoming more centred you co-operate and have the ability to choose your responses to difficult situations.

CHAPTER 8

UK LAW AND HOW TO BUILD A BULLYING CASE

What Is Law?

Law is a collective set of values and beliefs that have been decided upon in the high courts. The aim of the law is to protect you and your community from mistreatment and harm.

Some people hold the belief that "the law" is a strict solid line that you cannot cross, if you do cross it the whole world will come down on top of you. This is simply not true. Purely relying on the Criminal Justice System to solve your personal problems is a recipe for disaster. If you want to help yourself take all the advice in this book, but do not rely exclusively on the British legal system to solve your problems.

If you are serious about involving the courts then be prepared to attend court and give your evidence. The legal system takes time. If you make a formal complaint to the police and there is enough evidence to take your case further then be prepared to wait. In most cases it will take six months to get to court. In the case of domestic violence the court will fast-track your case as it 'is a greater priority.

A lot can happen in six months; the bullying may stop and you may feel that court is now not in your interest. It is your right to discontinue your case, but remember if you go back on your initial word and the bullying starts again, you will be in a trickier situation. If you are serious stick to your word and follow it through.

The Legal System Explained Simply

The Legal System can be compared to making a special film. The writers of the film's script are lawyers and judges. They decide what script will be used, and they write the law. You are an actor in the film, but you can alter the film's story. You have been involved in an incident and you contact the police. The police act as the film makers, and have a film crew, director and many assistants. They record what you have to say, they organise make-up artists and runners. The police take photos of what has happened, they contact other actors and record what they have got to say. They also interview the person who has bullied you and record what he has got to say.

The police make your film and present it to a Crown Prosecution Service (CPS) solicitor. The CPS solicitor edits the film and will decide if the film is of a good standard. The CPS decides whether the film can be released to the general public and then release it to the courts. The CPS, not the police, decides to prosecute your bully. The courts receive the film and the person bullying you has an opportunity to say if the film was recorded correctly and that they have been bullying you. If the person bullying you decides not to admit that the film was correctly made, he can then ask the court to play the making of the film.

The court watches the making of the film and then decides if the person bullying you has acted against the law. The judge or magistrate in the court then punishes the bully for breaking the law.

Criminal Law

The criminal law is used by many different agencies not just the police. This type of law is administered in a Magistrate's Court and Crown Court. Less serious offences are dealt with in the Magistrate's Court. The legal system requires a hefty weight of evidence and a case has to be proved beyond reasonable doubt. If the defence can instigate an element of doubt then the case can be disproved.

Civil Law

This type of law is easier to prove. The case has to be proved on the balance of probabilities. What this means is that if it is probable that the bully has acted in a certain way then the court can decide guilt based on his actions.

What Laws Can Protect Me?

There is not a UK law that protects you against bullying or domestic violence specifically. However, there are many laws that can be used depending on what has happened to you. Some victims may instigate proceedings in a criminal court or a civil court.

Offences Against The Person Act 1861 (Criminal Law)

- Common Assault
- Actual Bodily Harm
- Grievous Bodily Harm without intent
- Grievous Bodily Harm with intent

An assault is: any **intentional** or **reckless act** which causes a person to **apprehend immediate** unlawful force or **personal violence**.

Common Assault is the lowest recorded type of assault. As the seriousness of the injury and the intent of assault increases, so the type of law changes.

Offences under the Theft Act (Criminal Law)

- Burglary
- Robbery
- Theft

Miscellaneous Offences (Criminal Law)

- Blackmail
- Kidnap
- Racially aggravated offences
- Using violence to secure entry into premises
- Sexual offences
- Public order offences

I could write a whole book about all the laws that can protect you, including case law, background and legal arguments. That is the speciality of the legal profession. As a victim of bullying it would be better for you to learn about how to collect and present the story that you have experienced and then give this information to a legally trained solicitor or police officer. I can assure you that if you follow the advice in this chapter you will save yourself time and money. The whole process will be easier and less complicated and your bully will be more inclined to plead guilty at court. When you build a house you need the plans drawn by an architect, however, you also need raw materials and construction workers to build the house. In a bullying case you provide the raw materials and help provide some of the skills to build the house. The fully trained solicitor will provide the final plans. It is that simple. A lot of hard work is in front of you.

The police will arrest the bully and they will ask him to give his side of the story The police have strictly limited powers as to the length of time they can keep a bully at the police station (usually 24 hours) and they cannot impose conditions when forced to release him or her on police bail. The police only have the power to impose bail conditions on an arrested person following a charge. The decision to charge someone to court means that the CPS believes that there is enough evidence to prove that the bully has broken the law. The CPS also decides whether to drop the case.

The Protection From Harassment Act 1997

In 1997 legislation was introduced to tackle stalkers and also to provide more effective protection for abused women, in particular those who do not live with their abuser, than had been previously available. This legislation is perfect for bullying cases.

Criminal Offences Under The Protection From Harassment Act 1997

The Protection from Harassment Act 1997 introduced measures for protection under both the criminal and civil law, and also provides a link between criminal and civil law. The provisions include two criminal offences: the offence of criminal harassment (under s.2, a summary offence, tried in the magistrate's court) and a more serious offence involving fear of violence (under s.4, triable either as a summary offence, or as an indictable offence in the crown court). If convicted of either of these offences, there is an additional measure for protection: a restraining order can also be granted by the court, stopping the offender from further similar conduct.

Definition

Under s.2, (the offence of criminal harassment) a person must not pursue a course of conduct which amounts to harassment of another, and which he knows, or ought to know, amounts to harassment of the other, ie. if any 'reasonable person' in possession of the same information would regard such conduct as harassment. The term 'reasonable person' may be problematic in practice, but the aim of the legislation is to shift the emphasis from the subjective harmful intent of the alleged offender, which is often difficult to prove, to what actually happens and its effect on the victim.

A course of conduct includes: sending abusive text messages; following and stalking; sending abusive letters; placing abusive posters on the wall; spreading malicious gossip; sending threats; being overbearing; sending correspondence to a person etc.

Under s.4, (the offence involving fear of violence) anyone whose course of conduct causes another to fear, on at least two occasions, that violence will be used against them is guilty of an offence 'if he knows, or ought to know, that his course of conduct will cause the other so to fear on each of those occasions'. Although there are already powers under existing criminal law to deal with fear of physical violence, this new offence may be useful as it will allow the courts to deal with serious stalking without having to wait until psychological or bodily harm is caused.

A course of conduct, that causes someone to be in fear of violence, can be difficult to prove. You have to be very descriptive and the account that you give to the police has to be detailed.

The police can arrest without warrant anyone whom they suspect of committing either of these offences and the separate incidents do not have to be of the same kind each time. For example, shouting obscenities outside a woman's house on a Saturday, followed by a broken window the next Friday could constitute a related 'course of conduct' even though the conduct is different each time. Both could be prosecuted under existing legislation (for example as public order, or criminal damage offences) but would also constitute an offence under s.2 of the Protection from Harassment Act 1997. The police and the Crown Prosecution Service (CPS) would have to decide whether to take forward one offence or two. The advantage of going for the single offence of harassment is that it allows the court to hear the entire catalogue of incidents, the evidence for which may be weak individually but strong collectively.

A number of potential advantages include strengthening the options for police to protect you and to use the criminal law against bullies who continue to threaten and pester. Another advantage is that criminal proceedings resulting in a conviction under the Protection from Harassment Act 1997 will mean that a restraining order can be attached. Restraining orders can provide the same protection as injunctions under the civil law, but may be more effective as they carry stronger penalties. Lastly, action under the criminal law, coupled with restraining orders, may avoid the problem of the costs of legal aid for civil action.

What Do I Need To Do?

The law has the ability to protect you. However, the law is useless without the necessary evidence to support your version of events. How you record and present the evidence against your bully will have a dramatic effect on getting the case to court. This chapter will advise you about what to do and when to do it.

Making A Statement To The Police

The police will ask you a number of questions and to write a statement about what has happened. Check and sign the statement. If your statement has any inaccuracies make sure that they are changed and signed. You may have to be video interviewed. This is a procedure that provides the police with the best possible evidence. This evidence can be played to the court.

Tell the police exactly what happened, including what you saw and heard. Tell them if you fear for your or your family's safety. Tell them if the crime was made worse by abuse related to race, sexuality, religion or disability.

After you have made your statement the case is passed to the Crown Prosecution Service. The CPS decides whether there is enough evidence for a criminal conviction. The CPS applies a number of tests and considers if the matter needs to be resolved in a court of law. If the CPS decides that your case merits action by the courts the CPS will direct the police to charge the person bullying you. Once they have been charged to court you will be informed about the first hearing. In the meantime the police can impose bail conditions; these conditions are rules that are designed to protect you and the administration of justice. For example: not to contact you, not to enter your town, not to leave the country. If the bully contravenes these conditions, he can be arrested and put before the court.

The first hearing is an opportunity for the bully to plead guilty at an early stage. This has an advantage for both you and the bully. The bully gets less punishment and you do not have to give evidence and attend court. If the bully pleads not guilty then a trial date will be set by the court. You will have to give evidence and attend court. Most cases are heard in the Magistrate's Court. Jury trials for more serious trials are held in the Crown Court.

How Do I Strengthen My Case?

In order for you to be successful in court you have to give as much detail as you possibly can, and don't leave anything out. If you have been dishonest tell the police in the first instance. If you omit something from your statement you will undermine your case. Be honest. Never take matters into your own hands, as you will weaken your case and jeopardise your chances of a successful outcome.

Going To Court

The witness service and police will support you; if you are a vulnerable witness the police will assess this prior to you giving your statement. What this means is that the police and CPS will be able to apply to the court for special measures. Special measures are instructions that allow the court to become more people friendly. For instance a victim can request the following:

- Physically placing a screening between the witness and the bully in Crown Court.
- Evidence from the witness by live link (via a video camera) in Crown Court and Magistrates' Courts. You won't have to enter court and you won't see your bully.
- Evidence given in private in Crown Court and Magistrates' Courts.
- Removal of wigs and gowns in court (not applicable for magistrates).

The use of video recorded evidence in court paints a true picture. The jury will be able to see how frightened you were and will be able to identify with your feelings.

Victim support can arrange a visit to a court room; this will allow you to get a feel for the entire process. You will be appointed a victim care officer. This person will keep you updated about the case and will assess your individual needs. You may receive financial support with childcare arrangements, travel etc.

Ian's Story

This story is not a real life story, however, it touches on the type of harassment that you may encounter. The advice in this section will help you present your story in a clear light. When you contact the police or a solicitor they will take much delight in the lengths you have gone; it will really help your case.

I have included a copy of Ian's statement, and each section has advice and comments. It tells you what you need to do. When writing your own diary of what has happened Ian's statement will give you an idea of the detail that is needed.

Introduction

My name is Ian Davies and I am making this statement as I have been bullied and harassed by a person I know as John Cooper. I have had a long time to think about what has happened, and I am prepared to attend court and give my evidence if it is necessary. I wish to make a formal complaint of harassment to the police and I understand that this statement may be used in different ways.

Background

I am 18 years old and I am a student at Bridgend Comprehensive School. I am currently studying three A levels and hope to go on to further education. I attend school each week and I also have a Saturday and Sunday job at Somerfield Store, Bradford Road, Bridgend. I started work at the store six months ago. My duties include stacking shelves and working the tills. I work approximately 16 hours per week. The store employs local people and the majority of weekend workers are sixth formers. I work with some of my classmates. I work with the following friends: Jemma Edwards, Lucy Croft and Damien Bailey. We all work the same shifts and then go out with each other in the evenings. We all have a laugh and enjoy working together. At first the bullying was unnoticeable. I didn't think anything of it, and I just thought that John Cooper was a moody person. I have known John Cooper for six months. He works the same shifts as I do. Cooper is seven years older than me and has been working at the store since he left school. The harassment started three weeks ago. I have just started a relationship with Lucy Croft. We have known each other for years as we attend the same school. I recently asked Lucy to go out with me and Lucy agreed.

Within the first couple of days Lucy warned me about Cooper. Lucy told me that she had gone out with him for one year and that the relationship had ended three months ago. Although Cooper still works on the same shift as Lucy, he took the separation badly and there were a few problems between the two. Lucy wanted to keep our relationship a secret, however, people got to know about it and that's when the problems started.

Description

Cooper can be described as a white male, aged 25 years old. He is stocky and muscular in appearance. He is 5'8" tall. He has a Welsh accent. He has short brown hair, brown eyes and a tanned complexion. Cooper has a number of distinguishing features. He has tattoo on his right wrist that has "HELL OR HIGH WATER" written on it. Cooper has a slight stammer.

Incident One Introduction

On Saturday the 10 August 2008 at 8pm I was at work at Somerfield's. I was directed to work behind the scenes in the dry goods warehouse by my manager Sue Evans. The dry goods area is a large warehouse that stores all the dry store goods. It has a centre aisle and has large shelving units either side. The store area measures thirty metres by thirty metres. It is room that is well lit. At this time I was stacking the clothes aisle with my friend Jemma Edwards. For ease of understanding I have drawn a diagram of the layout of the warehouse. This diagram is not to scale. I produce this as evidence marked (ID/1), court exhibit (. . .).

What happened?

I was kneeling on the floor and placing clothes onto the shelves. Jemma was doing the same type of work. She was kneeling one metre away to my left-hand side. I was closer to the main aisle. There was no one to my right-hand side. We were talking about going out after work and Jemma was asking me about my relationship with Lucy. There was no one else in the warehouse. I could hear footsteps behind me and all of a sudden I felt a sharp pain to my head. I could hear a lot of screaming and I felt dazed and confused. I woke up and I saw Cooper standing above me. Cooper had a concerned look on his face and he was asking, "Are you alright? Are you alright?" I responded, "Yes, Yes." Jemma said to me, "You're bleeding. You have been cut." I could taste blood in my mouth and I placed my hand around the back of my head. I touched my head with my left hand and then looked at my hand. My hand was covered in blood. Cooper was in shock. His face was pale and he looked frightened. He said, "It was an accident, an accident." I said, "What happened?" Cooper said, "I was carrying some boxes and I slipped on a toffee wrapper and fell into you. I had nowhere else to go." As Cooper said this Mrs Evans came into the warehouse. Mr Evans asked what had happened and I explained. My injury was cleaned and a bandage was wrapped around my head. I was OK -- a little shocked, but OK. I had a small cut to the back of my head. I didn't see what happened.

What should I do?

At this stage you do not know if you have become a target. Take a picture of the area of where the incident happened with a digital camera. Make an official record of the incident in your company's health and safety book. Check to see that the other people present have made a statement. Get your injuries recorded by a GP. Make sure that all persons have signed their statements. Take a photograph of your injuries. Start and record this information in your own personal bullying diary. Consider drawing a diagram or sketch plan of the layout of the area.

Writing A Personal Bullying Diary

Make some notes before writing your diary. When you make your notes break each aspect of the incident into small sections. Put each section into small circles and apply the following questions: who, what, why, where, when, and how. Once you have answered each question move onto the next section. The smaller you break each part down the more detailed your diary will become. Once you have a plan stand back and leave it alone for a couple of hours. Return to your notes after you have been refreshed and repeat the entire process again. Now write your statement in small simple sentences. Remember to use descriptive words and do not leave any of the details out.

Include the following information in your personal diary:

- **Amount** of time (when the incident started and finished)
- **Distance** (how far you were away from the bully?)
- **Visibility** (what were the lighting conditions like; was it night or day; how well you could see the bully?)
- **Obstructions** (was there anything obstructing your view?)
- **Known or seen before** (how do you know the bully; when did you first meet them?)

Your diary should be kept in a safe and secure place.

Incident Two Introduction

The works canteen is situated in the centre of the store. It is a large room that has ample seating for 25 members of staff. The seating areas are divided into two rows. The main aisle runs down the middle of the two rows. The main entrance is situated directly opposite the serving area. To the right of the room are a number of whiteboards that are situated on the wall. The whiteboards contain staff information, items for sale and general notices. This room is the hub of the workforce and is a place where we all unwind.

What happened?

On Monday 12 August 2008 at 10 am I arrived at work and went to the male locker rooms. I got changed and put my works uniform on. I then walked from the locker rooms along the hall to the canteen. As I was walking to the canteen I saw my work colleague Diane Smith. I looked at Diane and said, "Good Morning." Diane replied and said, "Good Morning, Stripper!" As Diane said this she laughed and sniggered. I thought to myself, "How strange." I walked on and entered the canteen. I walked into the canteen and heard a loud wolf whistle. A group of female colleagues were sitting in the right hand far corner of the room. The women were sniggering and laughing among themselves. I was approximately ten metres away from the group. Standing next to the women and laughing with them was Cooper. I then stood at the end of the queue and waited to get served my cup of tea. To my horror I saw an A2 poster of a man completely naked. The man's body was superimposed and my head was placed on the man's body. The poster was very degrading as I was naked on the poster. At this point Cooper was standing five metres away from me. There were no obstructions in my view and the room was clearly lit. Cooper was the only person standing. He was wearing his works uniform. Cooper stood with stern authority; his chest was puffed up and looked directly at me. Cooper had a big grin on his face and was smiling at me. He pointed at me with his right arm and said, "Hey girls, he's a right stud." As Cooper said this he was making thrusting sexual movements with his hips. The women who were sitting next to him were laughing and pointing at my genitals. I was embarrassed and ashamed. I felt very upset and was totally humiliated. I turned around and walked out. I could hear all the staff laughing and this made me feel even worse.

What Should I Do?

Write a diary entry about the incident; include what was said, how it was said, and who was there, etc. Be as detailed as possible. At the end of the diary entry include how you felt.

Take a picture of the poster with your digital camera. Ask someone else to witness the position of the poster and ask the witness to sign their names on the bottom right hand corner. Make sure you include the time and date. Remove the picture carefully. Make sure you remove it wearing gloves and place it in a large envelope. Do not touch the poster or show it to anybody else. Record the time and date you removed the poster and sign the envelope accordingly. Give the poster a name. Write a dairy entry about the poster. You can draw diagrams or use maps/plans in order to illustrate your point of view. Do not react and take matters into your own hands.

Incident Three What happened?

I am the owner of a Nokia mobile phone operated by Easy Telecoms. The telephone number is 10987654321. On Wednesday 14 August 2008 I was at my friend's house watching a film. My friend's name is Jonathon Howe. At five past eight in the evening I received the following text message; "YOU ARE TREADING ON THIN ICE, IT'S GOING TO CRACK". I recognised the sender's number as Cooper's. I did not reply to this text message.

Whilst I was at my friend's house I accessed my email account on his laptop computer. I logged onto my account and I opened the first email. The email was sent by Cooper. The email read; "YOU ARE BEING WATCHED, BE CAREFUL, BE AFRAID".

What Should I Do?

Write out the text message on a piece of paper, sign and date it. It should read something like this: on Wednesday 14 August at 2200 hours I received a text message from the mobile number 12345678910. I know this to be Cooper's phone. It was sent to my phone number 10987654321. This mobile phone is owned by me and I am an Easy Telecoms customer. The text message said, "YOU ARE TREADING ON THIN ICE, IT'S GOING TO CRACK". I did not reply to this message.

Repeat the procedure with each text message. Ask a witness to read the messages and ask them to sign each statement. Save each message on your phone's SIM card. Remove the SIM card and keep it for safe keeping. Purchase a new SIM card and consider changing your mobile phone number. You also need to evidence how you have your bully's mobile phone number. Include when and where you exchanged mobile phones numbers.

Save the email on your computer or on a removable memory stick or CD. Print the email using your computer and show it to a witness. Keep the email somewhere safe and hand it to the person dealing with your case at the earliest possible time. Make a diary entry of what happened; include how you felt, and when you opened the email. Do not respond to abusive text messages or emails.

Incident Four Introduction

I live at 20 John Street, Newtown. I live at this address with my parents. Our family home is a semi-detached property. The entrance to our home is attached to a small lean-to porch. The driveway measures ten metres and there is a small garden in front of the main entrance. John Street is a busy road and is the main trunk road that enters Newtown.

On Thursday 15 August 2008 at 8 am I got out of bed and got dressed. I went to the bathroom and brushed my teeth. I then walked across the landing and walked down the stairs. The stairs are situated directly opposite the front door. I looked at the door and I could see that a small parcel was situated on the floor. The parcel was situated next to a number of envelopes. I bent down and picked the parcel up. I brought the parcel closer to my line of sight. I looked at the address label; the parcel was addressed to me. I shook the parcel and felt some contents inside. The parcel was wrapped in brown wrapping paper and was light. The parcel measured approximately 20 cm by 20 cm. I began to open the parcel. I looked inside and saw that a book was contained within the wrapping. I pulled out the contents and read the title of the book. It read, "One Hundred Ways To Kill Yourself". I just reacted and threw the book on the floor. I felt physically sick.

What Should I Do?

If someone sends you a package in the post be very careful. The parcel could be contaminated. Try to resist handling the item as you may lose vital forensic evidence. Do not let anyone else touch the item. Ring the police immediately and pass the item to the police. You could also take a photograph of the item, specifically where you found it.

Incident Five Introduction

At this stage I am really afraid and I am constantly looking over my shoulder. I have stopped going to work and I am very nervous that the situation may escalate. I have told Lucy that I cannot cope anymore and that I want to curl up and die.

On Saturday 17 of August 2008 at 8 am I was walking along High Street. I walk to the Post Office each morning and get the papers for my family. High Street is an old Victorian street that has old houses situated either side of the road. The street has six or seven shops positioned in the centre of the village. The store where I work is not far away. It was a clear morning; the sun was shining and there were quite a lot of people about.

What Happened?

I made my way into the post office and purchased some papers and some milk. I know the girl behind the counter. Her name is Donna Mason. As I was standing in the cue I was talking to my old scout master Neil Evans. He asked me what I was doing with my life and I explained. I left the store at 8.10 am and walked out of the main entrance. I looked around; I could see a man standing next to his bicycle. The man was approximately five metres away from me. To my left Neil Evans walked away from the entrance. All of a sudden I felt a tap on my left shoulder. I turned my body to my left hand side and I saw Cooper standing a metre away. He was virtually on top of me. I felt anxious and afraid. His face was red and he was staring at me. His front teeth were showing and his jaw and face were shrivelled and tense. Within a split second he lunged his neck forward and spat at me. I could hear a "thump" sound as Cooper pursed his lips together and ejected saliva from his mouth. I closed my eyes and instantly placed my hands over my eyes. I couldn't see. The saliva was all over my nose and right eye. It felt disgusting, and was in shock.

Cooper was shouting at me. He pointed at me with his left fore finger. His hand was moving in a stabbing motion and he shouted the words, "YOU'RE HAVING IT, YOU'RE HAVING IT." As Cooper said these words his face became redder, and was snarled and angry. Cooper's right hand was clenched into a fist. He was stamping his feet on the floor at the same time. His chest was inflated and his arms were splayed out. I could see the veins in his neck protruding and his upper body was tense and muscular. All of a sudden he pulled his right arm backwards and stepped forward in a swinging motion. Simultaneously he threw a full body hook punch. I saw a flash. I remember feeling pain to my head. I lost consciousness and woke up on the floor. I could see and hear a number of voices. Words and noises were swirling around me. Cooper had left the area. I touched my lower lip and I could feel a protruding lump. My right fore finger was covered in blood. I had sustained the following injuries: two dislodged lower front teeth, bruised and swollen lower mouth, including my gums and skin.

What should I do?

If someone has spat at you, you need to preserve the evidence. You could take a photograph of the saliva on your face. This is not always practical as the first thing you want to do is remove it. If you do remove it keep the tissue that has the saliva on it. Place the saliva in a brown evidence bag and seal it with black duct tape. Record on the bag who spat at you, the time and date. If there is blood on the floor or in a room do not clean it up. This type of evidence is best photographed. It may also contain the bully's DNA.

When You Contact The Police

Try and remain calm. Tell the operator the following information:

- Where you are and where you are going to
- The name and address of the person who has assaulted you (you might not know this)
- The injuries that you have sustained
- Where the bully has gone
- The description of the bully and what they are wearing
- If you have been drinking alcohol
- Your correct address and telephone number
- Briefly what has happened

Record the names, addresses and contact telephone numbers of the persons who witnessed the incident.

You need to get your injuries professionally recorded. Take a photograph of your injuries and make an appointment with your doctor or dentist.

If the incident occurred in a public place ask the police or enquire with the local council if the area is covered by CCTV. It does not matter if the actual incident was not captured on CCTV. CCTV will be able to prove that he was in the area, and this may prove valuable if he tells the police something different.

Being bullied is a daunting experience. You may have never called the police before and it can feel peculiar. You are not alone. When you meet the police officer explain to them what has happened and what you have done. The officer will be extremely thankful for the efforts that you have already taken. Believe it or not you will have saved them a great amount of work. Do not be afraid to ask questions and form a good positive relationship with the officer in the first instance.

CHAPTER 9

SOLVING SCHOOL BULLYING

When I started to research school bullying I trawled through many school websites and read many school bullying policies. A school adopts its own policy according to its own experience. There is not much consistency from one school to the next. Some schools tackle the issue head on and others have a policy that appears flimsy and inadequate. As a parent it would be easy to blame a school for its shortcomings and it would be very easy to blame the school for your child's bullying problem. Bullying is all our problem and we can all contribute to its solution.

The community approach is one that involves problem solving and actively encourages all sections of the community to become involved. By adopting this approach you not only solve your child's problem, but actively make the school a safer place to study and work in. This approach will benefit your child's education, improve learning and benefit the wider community. If you are in the process of meeting the head teacher this may be an opportunity to raise the issues of the problem solving approach.

The community model adopts the theory of cause and effect. If the causes responsible for bullying are identified and reduced, then the overall effect of bullying is reduced. Many parents that I have helped over the years focus on the punishment aspect of this model. Punishment is seen by many as the answer to the bullying problem. If the bullying did not happen in the first instance, then I am sure there would be no one to punish.

For the community approach to work the various stakeholders need to understand what is required of them and what they need to do. Communication needs to be open and transparent. In many policing activities this model has been proven to work and reduce crime. Each stakeholder's actions are interdependent and contribute to a safer community. After all the stakeholders have been identified they must be given an opportunity to answer all the questions below. An action plan that is specific, measurable, achievable, realistic and set within a time period must be adopted and communicated to all.

Focussing On The Victim

- Has your child identified a pattern of when and where the bullying is occurring?
- Has your child identified a safety plan that minimises confrontational behaviour?
- Has your child's safety plan been incorporated into your child's daily school activities?
- Who has your child told?
- Has your child written an account of what has happened?
- Has your child been offered a counselling session?
- Does your child understand what effect personal safety has on their own welfare?
- Does your child have a good network of friends?
- Does your child carry a panic alarm or mobile phone?
- Have you limited your child's internet and mobile phone access?
- Has your child been offered assertiveness training?
- Does your child attend school- or outside clubs?
- Are you considering sending your child to a self defence class?
- Has your child identified why they believe the bullying is occurring?

Focussing On The Location Of Bullying; The School Environment

- Has the school identified a list of Bullying Trouble Spots?
- How often are these Bullying Trouble Spots patrolled by school staff?
- Has each Bullying Trouble Spots been risk assessed? What potential for injury does this location have?

- Does the school have CCTV? Does the CCTV cover Bullying Trouble Spots?
- Does the school have mirrors that cover blind spots?
- Does the school have a Tannoy system?
- How do staff communicate when an incident occurs? Do staff carry radios?
- Have staff had violence and confrontation training?
- Are the streets adjoining the school covered by CCTV?
- Does the school have a school bag searching policy?
- Does the school have metal detectors?

Focussing On The Bully

- How are the bullies punished?
- What help are the bullies offered? Are they referred to a counsellor, anger management specialist or educational psychologist?
- Has the bully been offered diversionary activities that keep them away from the victim and his/her friends?
- Has the bully's class involvement been monitored?
- Have the bully's parents been contacted?
- Are there problems at home?
- What efforts have been made to separate your child?

Focussing On The Bystander

The bystander is indeed part of the overall problem. Within sports psychology it is a well documented fact that the bystander can improve or motivate a performer into a more competitive state of mind. This is also called social facilitation. This same effect can be observed at football matches or outside nightclubs when violence occurs. In many cases social facilitation increases the risk of violence and harm. If we do not focus and re-educate the bystander then how can we begin to attempt to reduce violence on the streets of the UK? The bystander needs to understand this theory and take responsibility. Schools need to educate parents and children.

- Have the bystanders been identified?
- Has each bystander been interviewed?
- Has each bystander received an awareness input?
- Does the school punish bystanders?

Focussing On The Parent

Prior to going to school you must do the following:

- Take a good look at your child. Is there anything that makes them an attractive target? Follow the advice in the chapter "Personal Safety"
- Does your child know its daily safety plan?
- Does your child have a mobile phone, quick lock and panic alarm ready?
- Does your child fully understand the process of confrontation and reducing verbal bullying?
- Does your child know its self care plan?
- Give your child 15 minutes of quiet time; consider a simple breathing meditation
- Tell them that you love them and that you will do everything to help them
- Remind them to tell someone and report any incidents.

As a parent it is all too easy to go straight to the head teacher and demand the bullying to be stopped. I would advise parents to talk discreetly to as many school workers as possible. Consider informing the local school's community police officer, police community support officer, neighbourhood warden, classroom assistant or playground warden.

Focussing On The School Response

- Is the issue of bullying incorporated into daily staff meetings?

- Does the school segregate year groups at playtime?Does each member of staff know which children are at risk?
- How are staff members informed about bullying?
- Who is designated as the school lead with regard to bullying?
- Which member of staff co-ordinates school patrols?
- What systems are in place to report bullying?
- How is bullying investigated by the school?
- Is there a gang culture at school?
- Is there a designated safe room at school (a place where children can de-stress and relax)?
- Does the school monitor social networking websites?
- Does your school have an acceptable behaviour contract?
- Does the school have a telling policy?
- Does the school have a peer support programme?
- Does the school keep a watchful eye at home time? Are children escorted on and off the premises?

Peer support programmes adopt a mentoring service to all children. Certain children are chosen and are trained to listen and support others. These may also be called "Buddy Programmes". This type of programme develops the buddy and the victim. Valuable skills are transferred, and the children feel valued and listened to.

"Telling schools" support the concept that bystanders should report bullying to the class teacher. This takes the onus away from the victim. It also takes away the fear of "telling tales". I support this approach because fundamentally it builds a sense of justice. Stepping aside from the school problem, if we cast our minds to the daily reports of serious crime within the media of the UK, we begin to realise that if it was not for witnesses coming forward to the police, supporting justice, then our efforts would be futile.

Focussing on Partnership Agencies and Improving Communication

- How often do the local police or police Community Support Officers patrol key trouble spots?
- Has the anti-bullying policy been shared with the community and local councils? What can they do to assist?
- Are all parents aware of the anti-bullying policy?
- How are other agencies involved in the anti-bullying policy? (I attended a catholic primary school and the local priest would help with listening and pastoral care.)
- How are all concerns communicated?

CHAPTER 10

WORKPLACE BULLYING

Bullying Policy

Not all employers have a bullying policy. There isn't a specific set of laws that apply to issues such as workplace bullying. A responsible company will have a policy written that aims to address workplace bullying. I have met many managers who sometimes hide behind the word "policy". Policy means "adopting a flexible way of doing something that works towards achieving a particular result". Policy is simply guidance. It gets complicated when guidance is mixed with actual law. This mix-up can confuse the employee. The employee needs to understand their legal rights and the employer's policy needs to distinguish between what the law says and what the employer is prepared to do. These two factors overlap.

The company may have had an experience of workplace bullying. A policy is then written in order to guide its staff in the right direction so that all employees benefit.

However, if an employee is acting in a discriminatory manner and the employer is not addressing the workplace bullying then they may be breaking the law.

There are many laws that cover issues such as sex discrimination, disability, age, paternity rights, etc. It may be that your bullying experience may involve elements of such behaviour. In order to highlight your case you will have to evidence such behaviour and provide documentary evidence. It will not be sufficient to say you believed you were being bullied. What has actually happened and how you perceive the bullying can sometimes overlap.

Depending on the industry that you are working in bullying may, to the employer, seem trivial. Some employers may try and wash over the problems because they do not see how they are involved in a bullying problem. This may hold true in a very macho male dominated organisation. As hard as it sounds try and be sympathetic. What you call bullying and what they deem as bullying may differ. You may need to help your employer and evidence what has been happening and how you believe you can solve the problem.

I would recommend that you advise your employer that you are being bullied and that you work together to try and solve the situation. Employers do have a duty to look after you but do not confuse duty with your own personal responsibility.

What Is Workplace Bullying?

Workplace bullying can be varied. The following descriptions may describe the actions of the bully.

The bully may constantly joke at you. They will mock you in front of work colleagues, and then tell you that you are being over sensitive when you confront them. The bully may become silent when you enter the room, making you feel uneasy. The bully will try and control your life outside work. They will tell you that you have to stay on until the job is finished; cancel your holiday leave or treat you less favourably than other colleagues. The bully will tell lies about you and spread malicious gossip. You will be excluded from the group process; told that your views do not count. When your work performance is satisfactory your bully will try and undermine your efforts. Your boss will say, "He was trying to motivate you," by forcing you into a corner. Everything you do will be knocked back and criticised. The bully will blow everything out of proportion and threaten you with legal action and possibly the sack. They will make up rules and tell you that it is policy. Your bully will hide behind the employer and blame the senior management team. The bully will glare, sulk and beat his fists on the desk. The bully will turn around the situation and try and persuade you that it was your fault.

How Can You Evidence Such Abuse?

Follow the advice in the previous chapter 'How to build a bullying case'. Keep every shred of evidence that you can. Be alert to emails, posters, pranks, text messages, etc.

What Are Your Legal Rights?

Dispute Resolution Regulations

On 1 October 2004 the Employment Act 2002 (Dispute Resolution Regulations 2004), called 'the Regulations' in this guidance, came into force giving new rights and responsibilities to both the employer and employee. All employers must now have minimum procedures for resolving grievances, disciplinary action and dismissal. When you start work with a new employer, he or she must give you within two months of the starting date a written statement of employment particulars, such as pay and hours, and this must include a note of the employer's disciplinary and grievance procedures. In particular the note must set out any disciplinary rules which apply to employees and tell you to whom you should go if you have a grievance. Under the new Regulations an employer and an employee must in certain circumstances, by law, follow these minimum procedures.

How To Raise A Grievance

Grievance procedures are procedures which enable you to raise any concerns you have about your job with management. These concerns could be about the work itself, your working conditions or about the people you work with. Your employer must, by law, tell you in writing what procedures you should follow at your place of work if you want to raise a grievance.

The first thing to do if you have concerns is raise the matter with the person specified in the grievance procedures, usually your line manager. If this is not possible, or if your problem is with that person, you should go to the next most senior person. Try to get the problem resolved informally at this stage.

Although these first discussions are informal, you may find it helpful to keep a brief note of any discussions you had, noting the date and time, whom you spoke to, and the main points covered. These will be useful if the problem is not resolved at this stage and you have to go on to more formal procedures. You should begin a formal grievance procedure if your employer fails to resolve the matter to your satisfaction. If you do not begin a formal procedure, you will not be able to make a claim to an employment tribunal that your employer has failed to honour your statutory employment rights. (This does not apply, though, if your grievance concerns dismissal, or disciplinary action short of dismissal that you agree was taken on conduct or capability grounds.) If you do have to take matters further, the grievance procedure has three steps:

The Written Statement Step 1

You must set out your grievance in writing and send a copy to your employer. If you have problems expressing yourself in writing you can ask for help at a Citizens Advice Bureau (CAB) or, if you are a union member, from a trade union representative.

Generally in the case of bullying your complaint must cover any type of discrimination on the grounds of: sex, age, religion or belief, disability, childcare, race or ethnic appearance, marriage or transgender, working rights.

The Meeting Step 2

When your employer has read your written statement he or she must invite you to a meeting to discuss your grievance. He or she can allow himself or herself a little time to look into your complaint but should not delay for an unreasonable amount of time.

You have a **right to be accompanied** to this meeting by someone who works with you or by a trade union official. The meeting must be held at a time and place that are reasonable for you and anyone accompanying you. If either of or you is disabled, the employer must take all reasonable steps to make sure that you have no problems getting to the meeting. You should attend the meeting. If for some reason you, or the person you have chosen to come with you, cannot get there for a reason which you did not know about when the meeting was arranged, the employer must arrange another meeting and you should attend it. Prepare carefully for the meeting and discuss the matter fully with anyone you have asked to accompany you. If there is anyone there you don't know, ask your employer to introduce them. Your employer should explain how the meeting will be held, who will speak and when.

Your employer should give you an opportunity to set your case out calmly and clearly, and if appropriate, to explain what you have done to try to resolve the problem informally. Be proactive. Use the opportunity to make some suggestions as to how the problem might be resolved. This will help you and your employer. Be concise. If you have any other grievances, consider if you need to raise them separately. After the meeting – not necessarily straight away – the employer must tell you what he or she has decided. If you do not agree with his or her decision, you have the right to appeal, and your employer should inform you of this.

What You And Your Employer Can Do To Resolve Workplace Bullying

First contact scheme

You are having a bad day at work and you want to get your problems off your chest. You do not feel like confiding in someone at the office, so you ring your company's first contact scheme. The scheme is confidential. You have an opportunity to get your difficulties off your chest and speak to someone at the end of a telephone. If your employer does not have such a scheme, suggest it to them.

Confront the bully

Meet the bully on friendly terms, be polite and to the point. Explain to them your point of view and ask them to stop. Do not raise your voice and try to remain calm.

Mediation

Mediation is the process by which a neutral third party assists colleagues in the resolution of workplace disputes to reach a mutually agreed outcome. Mediation works because it allows problems to be solved at the earliest opportunity.

The Bigger Picture

You may have other problems that are causing you concern for example: financial problems, marriage problems, a recent bereavement etc. Inform your employers about these issues. Does your employer have a trained counsellor? If they do have access to services, ask for them.

Risk Assessment, Health and Safety

Ask your employer to risk assess your current working conditions. I would advise this, as there may be other factors that may be the cause of conflict. Within the workplace there may be working practices that increase stress and anxiety. These hazards may be a contributory factor and increase the likelihood of bullying. This idea goes back to the cause and effect principle. It may be something very simple. Many staff can become moody and irrational when they are not properly fed and hydrated and do not receive adequate rest periods. Identify these issues and report them to management.

Move

Your employer may be able to move you to a different location or area of operation, this may help you avoid conflict in the short term.

Shift Changes

Your conflict problems may be resolved by a shift change.

Start your diary

Record all your received and sent correspondence. Start your diary and evidence all that has happened in a chronological order. Write a statement and take guidance from the previous chapter.

Seek professional help

Arrange a meeting with an employment law solicitor; take early advice.

Request an independent investigation

Consider requesting an independent investigation in writing. A suitably qualified person would be able to spot workplace problems and then advise management on a whole range of issues. The findings would be able to help all aspects of the company you are working for.

The appeal

If you feel that your grievance has not been satisfactorily dealt with, you should tell your employer that you are going to appeal. He or she must arrange a meeting to discuss this. The same rules apply to this as to the original meeting. It must be at a reasonable time and place and you have a right to be accompanied. If you do not appeal, but go straight to an employment tribunal with your complaint, any money you are awarded may be reduced by between 10 percent and 50 percent.

After the appeal meeting the employer must tell you what he or she has decided. This is his or her final decision. If you are still not satisfied, and you think that your employment rights have been infringed, you may have to take the matter to an employment tribunal.

How Does This Three Step Procedure Affect You?

If you do not follow them it could be serious. Unless you have first put your grievance in writing – and allowed at least 28 days to pass – you will no longer, as a general rule, be able to make a claim to an Employment Tribunal based on a grievance with your employer or former employer (unless your grievance is about dismissal). If the grievance, disciplinary or dismissal procedures have not been followed before the case goes to a tribunal, the tribunal will decide whether that is the fault of the employer or you. If it is you, any money awarded will normally be decreased by at least 10 percent and possibly up to 50 percent. If it is the employer's fault, any money awarded will normally be increased in the same way.

When It's Not Going To Plan

Your complaints may not want to be heard by your employer. There are many reasons for this lack of co-operation. After trying to co-operate and provide a solution you may be forced to make some tough decisions.

- You could withdraw your complaint and decide to leave the employer.
- You could go on the sick and claim that you were faced with workplace stress.
- You could accept the bullying and try and ignore it (highly unlikely).
- You could after time, and after trying to resolve the problem, decide to take your employer to an employment tribunal. Proceeding with an employment

tribunal can be stressful. You can take it upon yourself to pursue such a claim, however, it would be far easier to instruct a properly qualified and experienced solicitor.

Disciplinary Action and Dismissal Procedure: What Your Employer Has To Do

Company complaints can become very messy and it may be the case that the employer will try to dismiss you unlawfully. The company unwittingly involves itself in corporate bullying. If your employer is contemplating taking disciplinary action against you on conduct or capability grounds, or dismissing you, the responsibility lies with him or her to start a dismissal or disciplinary procedure. Your company's procedure mirrors the grievance procedure.

Your employer is required to send you a written statement of his or her reasons and to arrange a meeting to discuss it with you. If you disagree with the decision he or she makes after that meeting, you have a right to appeal, and your employer must arrange a further meeting. You must appeal to complete the procedure within the Regulations. If you disagree with what your employer decides to do after the appeal meeting, you may decide to make a claim to an employment tribunal. Before doing so you may wish to take further advice, possibly from your union representative if you are a union member or local your Citizens Advice Bureau.

The meetings

You have a right to be accompanied to any meetings to discuss your grievance, and any meetings about dismissal or disciplinary action which your employer intends to take against you. You may choose to be accompanied by someone you work with or a trade union official.

The written statement

Your employer must prepare a written statement of his or her reasons for considering disciplinary action or dismissal and send you a copy of it. Read the statement carefully. The statement should be clear and explain your employer's position. If you have trouble understanding it, discuss it with a workmate or a trade union official or take it to a CAB.

The hearing

Once he or she has sent you the statement your employer must invite you to a meeting to discuss the issue. He or she should allow you enough time to think about what has been said but should not delay the meeting for an unreasonable time. You have the right to be accompanied to this meeting by someone who works with you or by a trade union official. The meeting must be held at a time and place, which is reasonable for you and anyone accompanying you. If either of you are disabled the employer must take all reasonable steps to make sure that you have no problems getting to the meeting. You have a duty to attend the meeting. If for some reason you or the person you have chosen to come with you cannot get there for a reason which was not foreseen when the meeting was arranged the employer must arrange another meeting and you must attend it. Prepare carefully for the meeting and discuss the matter fully with anyone you have asked to accompany you. If there is anyone there you don't know, ask your employer to introduce them. Your employer should explain how the meeting will be held, who will speak and when. Your employer must give you an opportunity to set your case out calmly and clearly. Listen to what your employer has to say and give your side of the case. Be concise. The employer may dismiss or take the disciplinary action against you at this point.

The appeal meeting

After the meeting your employer must let you know his or her decision. If you want to appeal against this decision you must tell your employer. You must appeal to complete the statutory procedures. Your employer must then arrange a meeting to hear the appeal. Again you have the **right to be accompanied** to this appeal meeting by someone who works with you or by a trade union official. The meeting must be held at a time and place, which is reasonable for you and anyone accompanying you. If either of you are disabled the employer must take all reasonable steps to make sure that you have no problems getting to the meeting. **You have a duty to attend**. If you or the person you have chosen to come with you cannot get there for a reason which was not foreseen when the meeting was arranged, the employer must arrange another meeting and you must attend it. Prepare carefully for the meeting and discuss the matter fully with anyone you have asked to accompany you. After the meeting the employer must **decide** what he or she is going to do and tell you what it is. This is his or her final decision and if you are still not happy with it, and wish to continue, you will need to take your case to an employment tribunal.

What Is An Employment Tribunal?

Employment tribunals hear claims about matters to do with employment such as unfair dismissal. The Tribunals are courts, but have less formal procedures than the ordinary civil courts. Preliminary hearings, known as Pre-Hearing Reviews (PHRs), usually take place before a legally-qualified chairman on his or her own. Full hearings, which decide outstanding issues and conclude cases, usually take place before three tribunal members; the chairman, and two members who are experienced in dealing with work related problems. Usually one of these members will have a background in management and the other will have experience of representing employees.

How Do I Apply For An Employment Tribunal?

In order to start the process you have to complete a form called an ET1. You can get this form at an Employment Tribunal Office or via the Employment Tribunal website. After completing the form your solicitor will be asked to provide a detailed file of evidence. The file of evidence will include written statements from witnesses. Your employer will also submit a file of evidence. Once you get to the tribunal your solicitor will have an opportunity to read both case papers and ask questions regarding the claims that you have made. You will be cross examined and this can be a daunting experience.

By winning a tribunal you will have proved that your employer has acted out of ignorance. Your victory cannot be celebrated until the lessons learnt by your employer are changed and adopted. Your employer has to make that final decision.

CHAPTER 11

FURTHER HELP

I hope that reading "Bullied" has helped you understand the complex issue of bullying. All our worldly problems stem from our need to control and dominate others. Once you understand bullying you are better prepared to manage a bully's behaviour. You may also recognise that you too also exhibit such behaviours. Real strength comes from learning about our own shortcomings and overcoming them. Confrontation and violence are sadly part of our daily experience. Learning about the stages of confrontation and personal safety will allow us to keep ourselves safe from harm and more importantly allow us to guide others about such dangers. The practice of meditation and shifting perspective allows us to develop a greater form of happiness and release us from mental worry and aguish. It takes time – please be patient. There are many agencies that want to help you. By using such agencies in a holistic sense we will be able to find a solution to our bullying problem.

The writing of this book has come from the experience and kindness of many. The book is in its infancy and if you would like to share your personal solutions to your own problems you can do so by contacting the author. I have listed many partnership websites at our website www.the-bully.com. Please do visit our website.

Anti-Bullying Products From www.the-bully.com.

Defence sprays, panic alarms, relaxation CDs, books, voice recording products. All supporting leading charities.

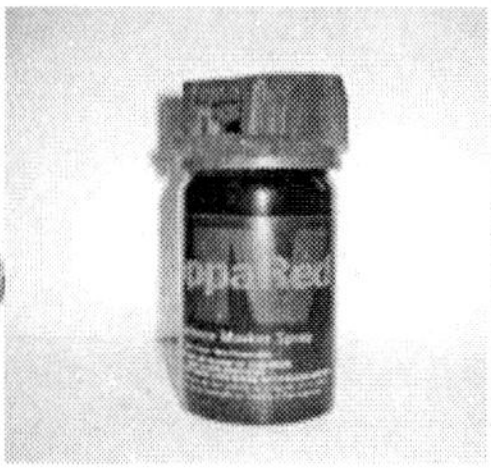

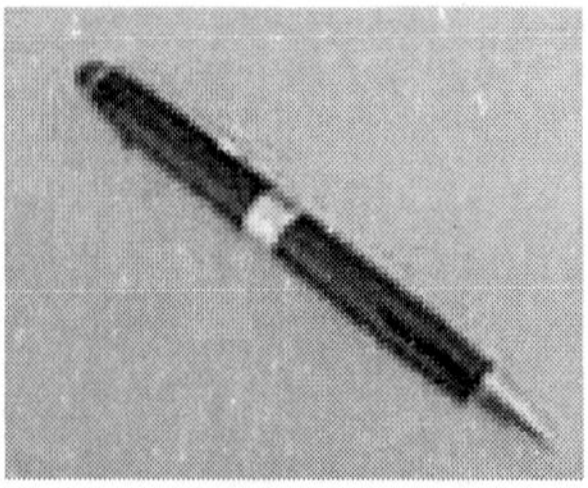